The Courage to Change

12 Powerful and Brave Stories
of the Courage to Transcend
Beyond the Darkness

Compiled by:

UCHECHI EZURIKE-BOSSE

My
Empowered
Living

Paperback ISBN: 978-1-9992039-0-0
Digital ISBN: 978-1-9992039-1-7

Table of Content

Introduction

by Uchechi Ezurike-Bosse

When I first decided to launch **The Courage to Change** book project, my main goal was to show people that they too have the ability to become authors, and they can also share their stories and lessons with others. I truly believe everyone has a story inside of him or her. Something unique to share that has the ability to impact and change lives. I wanted my authors to experience what I did when I wrote my book, 'From Aspirations to Fulfillment'. The satisfaction of knowing that my words, stories and lessons served and helped others. And so, **The Courage to Change** was born.

I put a call out for authors, and as Spirit would have it, 12 incredible women answered the call. These women I knew personally; some better than others. I have to say though, as I began to read their chapters and see their incredible stories through the pages of this book, I couldn't help but feel honoured and privileged to be able to share their stories with you.

As you read, you will see the power of courage. The courage to change and grow through painful and uncomfortable experiences. Courage to dare to dream of more, declare it and actually go for and achieve it!

I know as you read their beautiful stories, you too will be inspired to move through your current challenges. You

1

will see yourself in these pages through these women, because we are not alone in our journey. You will come to see that others have similar burdens and scars that may not be visible.

Oftentimes, we don't see and know what others have had to go through to reach their current positions. From these pages, you'll begin to get a glimpse of it.

It is my hope that as you read this book, you too will see that you have the ability to move past painful experiences, loss, trauma, doubt, and betrayal into forgiveness, acceptance and love.

It is said that courage is not the absence of fear, but the ability to show up despite your fear. To rise up and show up regardless of what is happening for you. Let this book be your catalyst of courage.

I thank you for having the *courage to change*.

Uchechi Ezurike-Bosse
Author, International Speaker, Strategist & Entrepreneur

LIVING
WITH GRIEF

The Courage to Change

4

Julie Brar

With 15 years' experience teaching yoga and meditation, Julie Brar has a keen interest in the mind/body connection for optimal health. She has four certifications as a yoga teacher including: Modo Yoga, Baptiste Power Yoga and Akhanda Yoga. Julie is also certified as a Health and Life Coach and holds a certification in Plant Based Nutrition from Cornell.

In 2012, Julie's husband died suddenly from a heart attack and subsequently, her world was turned upside down and inside out. Because of the sudden loss, Julie was in a state of shock for several months. Her health deteriorated as she struggled with sleep, joint and back pain, weight gain, skin issues, brain fog, depression, food allergies and adrenal fatigue. Ultimately, Julie was diagnosed with hypothyroidism and placed on medication. Though she went to multiple doctors, naturopaths, osteopaths and acupuncturists, her health failed to improve. She had gone from exercising and doing yoga several times a week to having trouble getting out of bed.

Because of her background in yoga and meditation, Julie believed there had to be a way to heal her body naturally. She went back to school for coaching and nutrition and used her yoga, lifestyle and nutrition knowledge to help heal her body. Over a period of four months, Julie lost 20 lbs, regained her energy, started to exercise and practice yoga. Julie believes that while healing from trauma can be a long road, with the right support it's possible to regain ones' health. She uses a variety of techniques to help clients regain their health such as nutrition, lifestyle changes, meditation and breath work; among others.

The Other Side of Love
by Julie Brar

Have you ever tried to make a deal with God?

On September 20, 2012, I tried.

God said, 'No.'

The day started beautifully. It was sunny; there was a bit of crispness in the air. It's one of my favorite Fall things, that crispness. I was in the middle of producing a play that was nearing the end of its run. Whenever I'm working on a play or a show I create a daily routine to keep me on track. For the term of the play, I would wake up every day with lists of producer things to get done. Things that I thought were the *most* important things. In a few short hours, all of those things would become unimportant and stupid.

After running through my usual list of emails about the show, I went to lie down because I had a massive migraine. I don't normally get headaches. Kim, my husband, had been out most of the day but he came home around two o'clock.

I went to take a short nap and asked Kim to wake me up at 3:30 so I'd have enough time to make it to the theatre across town. Being a low-budget indie production meant that, as the producer, I had the glamorous job of picking up wine and beer before the show so we could sell it between acts. I also got to run the box office. I didn't mind- what we were working on was so important that grunt work didn't bother me.

I had a pretty challenging director, which made my job as a producer harder than it needed to be. The thought of having to face her for yet another show was eating at me. But as they say, the show must go on.

Kim woke me up from my nap. My headache was marginally better. He gave me a nice long kiss. We had a chat about a job he was going to be starting in a couple of weeks. He counselled me on how to deal with my challenging director and then I made my way to the theatre on the Dundas streetcar. I did all my producer duties before the show. A girlfriend and her partner showed up to support the production.

We had a great show. I was originally planning to leave at intermission, but because my girlfriend showed up, I wanted to sit with her. I'd seen the show many times but spending time with my friend seemed like a fun way to pass the evening. Kim had made evening plans with a friend from Vancouver. I figured I might as well hang out instead of going home to wait for him. Usually, Kim and I texted each other when we weren't together but because I thought he was with his friend we didn't text.

After the show, I got back on the Dundas streetcar to make my way home to Cabbagetown. I chatted with someone from the show until he got off the streetcar. Then I called a girlfriend in Winnipeg to see how her kids were adjusting to the start of the school year. It was after ten o'clock. The sun was long gone. It was cold. I still had remnants of my headache.

I got off the streetcar all the while continuing to chat with my friend, our chat distracted me from my pain. I buzzed into our building and rode up the elevator. I unlocked the front door. The cat greeted me as she has a thousand times- all normal, usual stuff. Our cat, Sienna, is a rescue we got in Vancouver who we named after Sienna, Italy where we went for our honeymoon.

Kim and I had made a deal that we'd make it home after ten and watch Jon Stewart and share a bagel. Standard couple stuff, an occasional evening ritual. I didn't even take my boots off at the door. I walked right into the open concept kitchen living area, still on the phone chatting with my girlfriend.

I saw Kim on the couch. He was asleep with the lamp on. In a split second, it occurred to me that in all our years together I had never seen him fall asleep in that particular position. Something in my brain clocked his position. His guitar was on his body; his head tilted slightly back. How can anyone fall asleep with a guitar on them?

"I'm going to let you go. Kim's home; he fell asleep. I'm going to wake him up." My girlfriend and I hung up. I walked over to him and my heart immediately started to beat fast. I got a sinking feeling. He was blue gray. He wasn't okay.

My hands started shaking as my heart sank. I started gasping for breath.

I called 911. There was an answer right away but I couldn't get the words out. This is what a state of Shock is. But having never been in the state I didn't recognize it.

"Ma'am I can't hear you," said the Operator.

"It's my husband.... he's not breathing. He's not breathing..."

In between gasps, I got the words out. She instructed me to lay him on the floor to give him CPR. I started chest compressions and felt blood flow. The operator asked for my address. I knew the street number and our condo number, but I couldn't remember the buzzer number to get into the building. I told her to send paramedics to the concierge.

The flow of blood gave me hope. I started making deals with God.

"If you can fix this, if you can make him better, I'll be a much better person. I'll do more charity work... I won't take him for granted... I'll be less selfish.... I'll.... I'll do anything. Please fix this!"

There are some things that can't be fixed. No amount of praying or deal-making will work. This was one of those things. The paramedics came quickly, but to me, it felt like forever. The police also showed up. A female officer put me in the spare room and asked me questions about my evening. It only dawned on me later that I was being interrogated.

The lead paramedic kept coming into the room to ask me about medication, drugs, alcohol, and Kim's day. "Did he take anything?"-"Is he on medication?"-"What kind?"

"Yes," I answered. "Blood pressure medication."

I couldn't name the type or brand. What kind of wife can't name the medication her husband is on? I was gasping for breath the whole time, ugly crying, not caring about how I looked to anyone around me. The floor seemed to be opening up to swallow me whole. I wished it would. I wanted to trade places. I wanted Kim to be okay. I wanted to be swallowed up.

In my mind, I kept negotiating. "I'll be by his side all day, every day at the hospital," I was thinking to myself. I had started rocking myself on the floor. I was also running my index finger on a spot on my thigh. I did this until I managed to tear a hole in my jeans.

The lead paramedic came back into the room. "Where is his medication?"

I tried to answer the question, but my brain couldn't formulate the words. I tried to leave the room to show the paramedic where Kim's high blood pressure medication was but the officer held me back. No one wanted me to go out there to see. To see what? I don't know. Things were happening fast and slow at the same time. I had hope that as long as the paramedics were working on Kim, he would be okay. When the paramedics show up, don't things always turn out okay?

Not this time.

The fourth time the lead paramedic came in to tell me the news. "He was pretty far gone when we got here. We tried everything. I'm sorry." It took me a second to understand his words and then- PAIN.

Pain seared through my body in an instant. As he was telling me a part of my brain didn't want to believe his words.

How could this happen? I called the paramedics! It should all be okay! That's how it always is in the movies. Right?

Kim had been a part of my life for over eleven years. When I wasn't with him, I thought about him all the time in some part of my consciousness. But in a flash, he was gone. I felt like he was being pulled out of all of my cells at once. That was the PAIN I felt. My heart shattered into a thousand little pieces and I could feel shards of glass in my chest stabbing me. I crumbled to the ground. I wanted to scream and scream and scream until they had to tie me up. Instead I cried more. Snot dripped out of my nose.

My eyes hurt from the sting of tears.

The police wanted me to go to a friend's place. I called everyone I could think of close by and no one was answering. It was after eleven, most people were likely asleep. I ended up calling my friend in Winnipeg. The female officer wanted to know if my friend could come be with me. She couldn't. Of course not. She's in Winnipeg. When I told her the news, she was devastated. She had been at our wedding, stayed with us many times over the years. Out of all of my friends, she really understood Kim, his shy, quiet intellect.

Finally, I found a photographer friend who lived ten minutes away. He came over to watch me frantically pace, trying to figure out what to pack. Apparently, when someone dies in their home, the police have to conduct an investigation. How would I have known this? The things no one tells you.

Kim was still on the floor with a tube down his throat. My friend had never met him. This was the one and only time he saw him, with a tube down his throat lying on the floor.

They really had tried to save him. Kim didn't want to be saved. His Soul had decided today was the day. He left me behind and I didn't get to say goodbye. I had ten thousand questions for him that I thought I had a lifetime to ask. My time had run out.

I wish I had known we were close to the end.

In the hallway, they had started bringing out a stretcher. Their 'business as usual' was the end of my world. The female officer escorted us out of the building. It was dark. The ambulance had its lights flashing. There would be no rush trip to the hospital tonight. Everything had been moving in slow motion since I called 911. It kept moving in slow motion as I tried to digest the idea of Life without Kim. It was too big an idea. My mind refused to accept it.

"My dad passed away last year," the female officer said to me as a way of expressing she understood. She didn't understand. She couldn't possibly understand. Kim was IT. His was my FAMILY. We belonged to each other. Without him, where would I ever belong?

I spent the night at my friend's place. First, I called my challenging director and told her I wouldn't be back. They'd have to manage the show without me. The coroner called me at two-thirty in the morning to talk about conducting an autopsy. My friend patiently waited on me. Made me tea. Tried to soothe my broken spirit.

The coroner asked a big question. "Don't you want to know why this happened to someone so young?"

Of course, I wanted to know. I wanted to know why something this monumentally shitty happened to Kim. It wasn't fair. He was a good person. He deserved to live a long life. Though he hadn't always, he was taking better care of himself. My healthy habits had rubbed off on him over the years. Kim was even meditating to bring down his stress levels. He really was trying to stress less. I wanted to know why God had decided his time was up. I wanted answers.

The next few days were a blur of activity. Pain had become my new normal. My body hurt all the time. My heart still felt like shards of glass in my chest. My body refused to relax long enough to fall asleep. Friends flew to Toronto to help me with the funeral arrangements. I had to tell his family that he was gone. I had to tell his friends. I had to call the company he was supposed to start working for and tell them that he was no longer here.

In my mind danced a thousand memories of us together in a random twenty-four-seven painful loop as if to say, "See! This is what you won't have anymore! Bet you're sorry now you didn't appreciate him more." Every memory we had made together wanted to flood to the surface to remind me how much I loved him, love him still. The memories punctuated his absence and made every breath painful.

We had been making plans. Plans to buy a house and stay in Toronto. We had moved from Vancouver because Kim wanted to be close with his family here. I felt guilty I had cheated them out of time with him, all those years we lived on the West Coast. I thought we had time. We didn't. Turns out those years were his final years. He would never get to spend more time with his mother, his brother, his sister, or our nephews. Those years where I had him all to myself in Vancouver were years I stole him away from his family.

Kim was going to work for a start-up that he was passionate about. Maybe we would finally start trying to have a baby. I had been resisting for years thinking that I should wait for my acting career to get to a certain place before we got pregnant. We had finally agreed that it was time to start.

None of those things would happen now.

Instead, I planned a service with the help of Kim's brother and sister. Kim's mom let us do whatever we felt Kim may have liked. I want to believe that Kim would be proud.

Kim's brother shared funny stories about Kim growing up. His sister shared a moving tribute. I said nothing. I knew I couldn't speak without screaming and falling apart. I sat crying and watched the slide show that we had put together for the service. Pictures of Kim from when he was a kid, when he used to race triathlons, our wedding, our life on the west coast. Many memories. No more Kim.

I wasn't in Grief yet. I was still in a state of Shock. I went through the motions, doing what needed to get done. Even after the funeral and for weeks after I would stay in Shock. I stopped sleeping or eating properly. Some days I ate chocolate, drank wine and spent most of my day in the bathtub. Sienna would follow me from bed to bathtub and back to bed. Considering that cats like to sleep eighteen hours a day my new routine suited her just fine. The odd time I wasn't in bed, Sienna would hang out on the spot where I found Kim on the couch. She would clean herself, sleep and watch me from that spot. When I went back to bed she'd follow me back to bed. This routine lasted for weeks after Kim's funeral.

My friends went back to their husbands and kids right after the funeral. That was the worst. After the funeral. Everyone else had closure, but my life was ripped wide open. I was left trying to make sense of the tragedy. When people would see me in public they would give me pitying looks that would make me want to fly into a rage. They would say things like "Don't worry you're young. You'll meet someone else."

I got so angry. I didn't want to meet anyone else! I wanted Kim. I wanted to hold onto him. I could feel him beside me all the time but I couldn't get to him. It made me crazy.

The dumb things people say after someone dies. "Call me if you need anything." I got this from a lot of people. I need my husband to be alive. Can you bring him back? You can't? Leave me alone.

Sometimes people would ask, "Do you have kids?" As if not having kids made the loss easier. It didn't. It made me regret not having his child. At least if we had a baby together I'd have a part of him with me. Instead, I was left with clothes, books, pictures and memories. I didn't even have many of his physical possessions. In strange Divine timing, Kim had given away many of his worldly possessions when we moved from Vancouver. He had said he wanted to get new clothes when he got settled in Toronto. I feel on an unconscious level his Soul knew he was leaving. Where he was going required no possessions from him and so there wasn't much left.

I thought about killing myself. A LOT. Every day. Even when someone was sitting across from me trying to cheer me up. A part of my brain would hang out in deep dark places plotting my own demise.

I reread *The Year of Magical Thinking* by Joan Didion. I had read it when it first came out a few years prior. I was touched by the poetry of the book but the story never pierced my heart. I didn't cry then. I cried now. I understood. I didn't want to understand. I wanted to flip a switch that would bring me back to who I was before. Before Kim died. I didn't want Kim to be dead. I wanted it all to be a horrible dream that I woke up from. Every morning I woke up and had to adjust to my reality- *no Kim, only me, alone.*

I read other books on grieving. Some gave tips. One of them talked about getting into a routine. I didn't want routine. I wanted to have my multiple baths a day, chocolate and wine. Most of my casual friends had stopped checking up on me. Some of them had out-right dumped me because I wasn't back to normal, or at least the normal they were used to. It made losing Kim extra painful because now I was experiencing losses on top of loss. My Vancouver friends kept calling and texting me but they were in Vancouver and I was in Toronto alone. I hadn't been here long enough to forge deep friendships so as a consequence, most of those new friendships went away. One by one, dealing painful blows to my fragile heart. Every. Single. Time.

I didn't kill myself even though I wanted to. I thought of all the ways I could do it. No one would know. It was only Sienna and I. In the end I didn't want to hurt my friends. Some days that was the only thing that kept me from following through. Having just lost Kim, I didn't want to have others experience what I was going through.

There was one other book that helped me. *A Widow's Story* by Joyce Carol Oates helped me to understand that what I was feeling was normal. After losing a spouse, it's very normal to not want to keep living. In fact, there are many stories of couples who have been married for decades dying within a year of each other. I have a friend whose aunt and uncle passed away at the exact moment of one another. Reading *A Widow's Story* made me feel better but I was still stuck in shock, not even on the pathway to processing Grief. It also pissed me off that both Joan Didion and Joyce Carol Oates were married to their husbands for decades before they died. I was jealous. Maybe I'd be less angry, less suicidal if I had spent my whole life with Kim.

My mind kept dancing to the past. I thought of all the times that I had lost my temper or hadn't been the kindest to Kim. Now he was gone. I felt like a massive asshole. Mostly I missed him like one would miss breath. I didn't have any family. He was my family. Without him I was no one. I mattered to no one. If I went away it wouldn't be long before people would just go back to their lives.

I decided to do ten days of silent meditation four months after Kim passed away. My thoughts were driving me crazy, my body hurt all the time, and I couldn't function. There seemed to be an expectation by everyone around me that after a couple of months, I should be back to normal. The best I'd ever felt was after a ten-day silent meditation, so that seemed like a good idea. Against the advice of friends I made my way to the Vipassana Center outside of Barrie, ON.

Getting to the center was sheer effort. I didn't have a car. I had to take public transit to get as far north as I could.

From there, a volunteer would pick up whoever needed a ride and deliver us to the retreat center. My body was in extreme pain. Lugging my suitcase up the steps of the GO train bus terminal was excruciating. I willed myself to do it though an older Jamaican woman helped me part way up the stairs. My photographer friend had agreed to check up on Sienna and spend some time hanging out with her.

I was convinced that Vipassana could help me get a handle on myself. It could help me think straight again. Once there, they separated men and women. Everyone was given a place in the meditation hall. That was your spot for the entire ten-day course. We weren't allowed to make eye contact, talk, write, read, use a phone or do anything that can be viewed as contact. If you had a question about the meditation technique, you could ask the teacher during question period. But otherwise there was nothing but silence.

I checked in, got my room, organized my things and then waited for the course to start. I spoke to few people except those running the course. I wanted to get my safe space in the meditation hall. Time slowed. My thoughts were wild as usual. Finally, we got called to the meditation hall. I got my place and waited as everyone else was placed in the hall. This was my fourth ten-day silent retreat. Usually, older students are placed at the front of the hall and newer students go behind them in neat, perfect rows. That's how it starts. With each inner demon that each individual confronts in their mind the rows get more and more disorganized. As soon as everyone sat down, they dimmed the lights. The opening chant started.

PANIC.

My heart was leaping out of my chest. I started to sweat. My eyes flew open.

I couldn't stay here.

Kim.

He was everywhere. I felt him everywhere and nowhere at once. He wasn't with me. I wanted to scream. There wasn't a second of the day where I didn't think about him. Missing him was driving me crazy.

I made myself stay. I let myself cry on my meditation cushion, on the walks to and from the dining hall to my room and back day after day. I let myself face Grief head on. I let myself sink into the pits of despair. I faced darkness head on. I struggled the whole retreat. Never for a second did I feel Peace. My meditation sessions were battles in my mind where I fought to stay on my meditation cushion and not run around the room screaming.

Somehow I got to the end of the ten days. I was far from feeling great. But I had finally started to sleep again. I had graduated from Shock to Grief. I could finally start to wrap my head around going on with Life without Kim.

Grief is a whole other ball game. It was a road travelled in many small steps. The conventional year of mourning doesn't actually respect Grief for what it is. Grief showed up in unexpected moments and knocked me to the ground. It came in waves and over-took my body. Tears flowed with abandon. I couldn't plan my days.

Every attempt I made at routine failed. A couple of weeks after Kim's death, I started speaking with a therapist. It helped, but along with therapy, I knew I needed body workers. I created a team of healers: massage therapists, acupuncturists, osteopaths in Toronto and Vancouver that I saw weekly depending on which city I was in.

I went back to Vancouver three times in the year after Kim's death. It was always painful when I was there. Every corner of the West End reminded me of Kim. Memories of restaurants we used to frequent, coffee shops I knew he went to during work hours, memories of dinner parties we used to throw. In my first two trips back to Vancouver, I had frequent panic attacks. I had to leave or skip events because I couldn't calm my body down. After my meditation retreat, the panic attacks started to subside.

Grief kept revealing itself to me slowly. Every time I thought I was starting to get better, I would fall back. I lost more friendships, which didn't help.

Sometimes, I took two steps forward and a thousand steps back. I became depressed. My adrenals shut down. My thyroid stopped functioning. I put on weight. I couldn't exercise. I wanted desperately to get my life back on track but felt unable to stick to any routine that would get me there.

Being in therapy helped, but my body became a puzzle. I went from one practitioner to another to try and fix myself. I lived with chronic pain that made being physically active impossible. When Kim was alive, I worked out five days a week and did yoga almost everyday. Now I could barely walk some days. It seemed that even though I wanted to move on, my body kept pulling me back into Grief.

My dance with Grief was not a clean one. It was ugly and ungraceful. I was a mess. For YEARS. The books talk about the year of firsts. The first anniversary, birthday, Christmas without the person you love and how hard those events are.

I survived the first year but in many ways the second year was worse. In the second year, my memory of events started to fade. I felt like I was betraying Kim's memory by not being able to recall every last second of his final day or our time together. Then there is the reality that for many others, Kim is a distant memory. The door closed for them after the funeral. For me, that was the start of a whole other journey. I thought about him every day. Even after all these years, I still think about him every day.

A big challenge of the second year was that I met someone. I felt so guilty for being with someone new. Being with someone new didn't mean that I loved Kim less. My heart expanded to bring this new person into my life but I still felt guilty. No one told me that it was okay to be with someone new. Eventually, I found a way to make my peace and find joy in being in a relationship.

Health-wise I was still struggling. Extra weight, thyroid issues, back and joint pain kept me on the sidelines of life. I seemed incapable of moving forward.

The more practitioners I saw, the more frustrated I got. My body wasn't healing fast enough. My spirit was still broken. I felt terrible for not being a better girlfriend for my new love.

There's something I didn't understand while I was eyeball deep in Grief. No one told me.

It's okay.

It's okay that it's messy.

It's okay that I didn't go back to business as usual.

It's okay that I was okay one minute and falling apart the next.

Grief is a life long road.

I started to feel better slowly with each passing year. There was no moment where I was over Kim. I learned to live with Grief.

Even now I have days where it hits me like a brick. It's seems unfathomable at times. I didn't imagine him. He existed. Though many aspects of him are fuzzy in my memory. I used to be able to hear his laugh, the one he had at dinner parties. One day it faded away into the ether. Now try as I may I can't conjure it up. Why didn't I think to record it? Why ask why? It opens the wound, causing more pain. By now I've had my share. Grief is the other side of Love. No one grieves deeply unless they love someone with every fiber of their being.

Meditation became the bedrock of my daily self-care. Self-care isn't some hippy-dippy new-age concept. It's about preserving one's own well-being in order to handle the blows that Life gives all of us. Meditation became the container by which I could process my physical and emotional pain and move through it. It's a daily practice.

Over time, I added more modalities to help me heal. Tapping is a quick and easy technique that I use most days to keep energy moving. I've noticed stress hits me much harder than before Kim's death. Knowing that, I'm much more aware of taking care of myself.

There are gifts that came out of that awful day. Loss and Grief have made me a more empathetic person. I can hold space for other people's suffering in a way I never could before. That day exposed to me how fragile life is. One second we're here and the next we're gone. All that remains are the memories we make with the people we love. Hopefully our loved ones cherish us until the day they take their last breath.

That day made me change direction for my life's work. I promised myself the day of Kim's funeral that I would do something positive with the awful experience of losing him. I became a health and nutrition coach with the hope of helping others become healthier.

I was my first client. I had to help myself get back on track.

When I felt well enough, I began to move more. In 2015, I started back to a semi regular yoga practice. There were weeks where I didn't practice but over time I became more consistent. I had a lot of chronic joint and back pain. I had my team of massage and osteopaths that helped me when things got really bad for me physically. Being that aware and committed to improving my health meant that eventually, I did manage to get there. It wasn't overnight. There were many setbacks and restarts.

By 2018, I was able to work out consistently because the pain in my body was gone. I was finally ready to tackle my weight. In truth, it was less about my weight and more about how I felt in my body. I wanted to feel strong and healthy again. I missed the strong fit Julie. Now I was ready to dive in. It's okay that it took me six years to get there.

When I got the autopsy report a few months after Kim's death, I finally found out what happened on September 20,

2012. Kim had a type of heart attack called the Widowmaker. Only 20% of people survive. His fate was decided decades ago.

Unfortunately neither one of us knew this. I believe, on some level, Kim's Soul chose to go that way, on that day. His father had heart disease complications; which lasted for years and affected his quality of life. Kim said he wanted to go quickly. When someone has a Widowmaker heart attack they don't feel any pain. One second they're here, the next - poof- gone.

That night taught me it's not that God wasn't listening. It's that my purpose for this Life is bigger. Kim's heart attack became the catalyst by which I could be reborn. I had to want it and work for it though. No magic tricks.

I had to learn who I am capable of being. Losing Kim was the start. Not the end.

A tragedy can derail you or push you to become better. Life is always happening *for* us, not to us. This is hard to recognize when big life events happen. I chose to rise and become stronger. I now know how fierce I am.

My purpose isn't to make movies, write stories, coach clients or teach a good downward dog. I can do all those things, but my true purpose is to chip away all that blocks me from myself and Love. And hopefully show others along the way that it can be done. God has not forsaken them.

Overcoming my own health challenges has taught me to take my health seriously. I pay attention in ways I never did before.

Realizing how finite and fragile Life is made me passionate about living. I became grateful for the Life I have been gifted with. There are no stops or do-overs. It's all happening NOW.

God *was* listening.

Cheryl Roberts

Cheryl Roberts is a Mother, Wife, Entrepreneur, Corporate Manager, Community Member and Leader. Cherly is a graduate of University of Toronto and holds an Honours degree in Management and Economics along with Sociology. She is also an Alumni of the Smith School of Business at Queens University.

Professionally, in the insurance industry, Cheryl strives to offer what she's learned and serve people by helping lives, families and businesses just like you especially in your times of need.

She is the Owner and Independent Insurance Broker of Cheryl Roberts Life and Living Benefits representing 20 plus Companies who offer various products and services for all your insurance needs.

Cheryl is also the Regional Western Ontario Manger for McDougall Insurance and Financial Brokers where she manages a team of 60 people and 4 branches to offer you solutions for your Home, Auto, and Business insurance needs.

Cheryl loves what she does because she offers specialized services and will be there when you need it most; while living through a claim. She has personally seen how unexpected events affect people and families and is dedicated to being there and assisting families to navigate through those times with ease.

Her goal personally is to be able to be the best version she can be, and to inspire her children and family to be the same for themselves leading with love, kindness, strength and courage by living that example.

As a leader in the community, Cheryl hopes to inspire others to be true to themselves and help others reach their potential whatever that may be. Dreams can happen with hard work, courage to fail and get back up again, determination to keep moving forward no matter what life throws at you and perhaps a little luck of the stars to go along the ride.

The Transformational Truth about Living with Love and Loss
by Cheryl Roberts

Know that moment in life when everything changed?
Not just the gradual change from childhood to adulthood; or
the transition into a new career. Not the difference of living
alone to living with your partner/spouse; or having no kids to
having one, two or even three. Can you conjure the feeling of
love- unconditional, true, and real? Have you ever lost love
or experienced the moment when it just died? That moment
before death and that exact moment after?

I have.

The moment I lost my mother to an unexpected and very
quick battle with cancer, life changed. The only way to
describe it at that time was: blindsided. I wasn't sure what to
do next. What I also didn't bank on, after the shock of it all,
was that my life would never be the same in so many ways.
Everything changed and challenged the views I'd lived the
first part of my life knowing to be the truth. My life changed;
the meaning of things changed, and the hero in this story
didn't win. I used to say things like "everything happens for
a reason", or "God won't give you more than you can
handle", and "this too shall pass". *This too shall pass?* Note
to future self, for the times I've said these things to people
experiencing the loss of someone they love; try not to say

those things right away. Perhaps wait for some time to pass before using words of wisdom that once made sense.

Loss has a way of turning your thoughts and your heart inside out and upside down. Things that made sense before don't have the same truth or power. Time suddenly felt like a commodity I could touch. It stood still in the moment I felt the loss of someone I so dearly loved. The truth however, is that time and life didn't stop. Time keeps on going and life kept on moving- with or without me. Those same phrases that kept me going during other hard times before now, seemed to live with a whole new meaning. A whole new life with loss that had now become *my new normal.*

Within this new life, one of my biggest fears is that I feel alone. But the truth is, I am not alone. I've had so many people in my circle, my tribe, and my family who are also watching this all unfold, and feel this loss as well. People who knew me, watched me suffer and yet needed me to *be me.* The *'me'* that they knew. Living with loss affects everyone. People wanted that carefree, full-of-spirit, kind, caring, motherly woman they always knew me to be. It's understandable, as no one ever asks for tragedy to happen.

In the early stages of my loss, I tried not to be hard on anyone that tried to use comforting phrases, even though they made me feel mad or sarcastic or even sadder. The people in my life were hurting too. People are often conditioned to find the good that should come out of bad times, even when you can't see it yourself. Yes, good things can evolve. Yes, perhaps there is a bigger meaning out of a poor circumstance; however, that doesn't just make it feel better. So how do any of us navigate through the weeds and continue feeling right within ourselves to live and love again, especially when you also know how hard it can be to deal with losing love over and over again? To experience pain through loss only means we have lived and loved.

I have loved. I have been loved. And I will continue to love.

I grew up surrounded by a huge family, and was blessed to know what true, unconditional love feels like. I know this to my core. So, when this love was suddenly taken from me- and by a disease so out of my control- I was left afraid, and with a feeling of unimaginable loss and deprived of the way I thought life would be. My recent loss happened within the past six months at the time of writing this. I struggle to even get this story into words. Yet, I am strangely inspired to do so.

My mother was a seemingly healthy 70-year-old woman, running around playing with my kids one day, to suddenly being diagnosed with stage four cancer with no qualification at that point for a cure. She was terminal and had one month left to live. We indeed lost her in one month. In the mess of what life has now become after losing my mom, I share this story of her teachings of self-aspirations. For me, for you and anyone who has been there too. I hear her speak those words to me now. *You are brave. You are alive. You are vulnerable. You've had enough. You are enough. You can and are breathing. Just breathe. Pray. You're not the first and you won't be the last person this has happened to. Breathe. Live. Love.*

I have decided to write this journey of love and pain with truth. I write this, and for one of the very first times in my life not at all for recognition, not for fame, not for acceptance, not to fix me or fix you, not because I was told to, but because I am thankful to be able to share my words. I watched my mother in her last days see so many people she loved come to the hospital, but with the cancer and medications she had no voice to speak. I saw the pain in her face as she still had so much she wanted to say, looking at us to be her voice and hoping we knew what she might be feeling or thinking in her heart. But by that time, it was too late. Too late for a woman who wanted to share her stories even if it was over and over again, each time she met people. Yet now she had no voice and perhaps could only hope that we knew her and her heart well enough to speak for her in her last days. At the end of our days, I suppose it's all we can hope for.

Hope that we have touched and inspired people enough that when we leave this physical world, our love is still felt by those who remain. I am here today and grateful for the gift of a voice. What I've realized is that pain, like love, needs a form of expression. It is very contrary to social acceptability however, to express pain and live with pain. Most see pain and suffering as an uncomfortable feeling or an illness that one needs to get over or fix. At times, it may just feel easier to say they are ok. I write this to share the real-life story not many have the courage to tell you about.

Sometimes we may need validation in life that what we feel is normal and that's ok. What's more important is to share and support each other. My story may not be unique, but how I tell it is. No one needs to suffer alone; your voice is also your gift. Maybe others may want to tell their stories too. It is a story that I wish my past-self had read a long time ago- a story that I appreciate so much more now as a Woman, a Mother, a Wife, a Sister, a Daughter, a Niece, a Friend, a Neighbour, a Community Volunteer, a National Corporate Manager, an Entrepreneur when dealing with love and death.

I love people and thoroughly enjoy hearing about the stories and lives of others. I am an "anything for you" type of person. When I feel, I don't hold back. When I hurt, it can be physically painful. When I love, I love with all of me. Some of the biggest moments in life where I experienced loss were twenty years ago losing my first love and ten years ago after losing my Grandmother, the only grandparent I knew and who was more like a mom. It was also ten years ago that my husband and I lost our first baby at four months prenatal. And then six months ago losing the person who brought me into this world and gave me life: my heart, my mother.

If you have experienced loss of love through grief, here are a few things I have learned the hard way and in a short period of time. Grief is not a disease with a simple cure, nor do you have to "get over it". Your heart and your mind are rearranging life to make sense of it all. Be patient and kind to yourself as you go through it. When dealing with the anxiety that comes along with loss, you won't always get what you need in life to feel protected. But to feel safe again, ask yourself what it is you need in those moments to feel better, and try to do it. Believe there is gratitude for the good and bad that can happen in your life journey.

Author Megan Devine, in her book; '*It's OK That You're Not OK: Meeting Grief and Loss in a Culture that Doesn't Understand*', describes early stages of loss as "Your mind is trying to keep you safe. Do your best to soothe your hardworking, overworking mind when you can. Tell yourself the truth about your fears. Ask. Listen. Respond. Commit to caring for yourself inside whatever comes. Above all be kind to yourself."

So often we hold back what we want to say when it comes to pain and loss. It gets stuck in our heads and we swallow it down to the pits of our stomachs. We allow the plaque to build up around our hearts and the weight of it to push on our shoulders. We doubt that what we feel is valid, that anyone cares or that it even makes sense. We doubt our ability to be strong or that we will have the courage to change. But why as a society are we so afraid to speak exactly what we feel?

The struggle to get here though is real. I get it. Trust me. I was raised in a Caribbean family where I was severely punished for not telling the truth in some circumstances, but then encouraged not to tell too much to certain people, even if it was the truth. I never realized then that the ideals I was raised to believe to be true might not end up being *my* truth. Complicated much?

The world needs "different strokes for different folks" and more people who are not willing to conform, and can be strong enough to tell their truth without fear whether they are sharing the good or bad things in their lives.

For balance, we need both the good times and the bad. However, from a very young age we are taught in our children's stories that are passed on from generations before, that if you do 'good' and be 'good', then 'good' things will happen. The hero always wins in the end, right? Good will conquer over Evil.

This idea is further ingrained in us through our education. When you do good work, you will get As. Anything less means you didn't work hard enough. So, you either make it to the top or get left behind. For me, report card day felt like I was at the mercy of my teachers' and my parent's judgement. What would they think of me? I focused on being the best because that meant that I'd made it. Everyone would be happy and proud. At least that's how I felt.

Hollywood, as well as Bollywood, has made billions of dollars selling stories of good vs. evil. The hero will win by the end of these two or three hours. There will always be a happy ending. The heroine will marry her hero. I applaud anyone who dares to produce a true story or screenplay that goes against the grain and may not have a happy ending. There is a need and much value in depicting the balance between good and bad times.

I wish the stories that we were told and the lessons they were supposed to have taught us, also showed us how to overcome obstacles when good didn't seem to win in the end. I wish they had shown us more of the truth and how to go on with courage and bravery. People experience loss and grief every day, the same way they experience love and birth. We need more of the truth. I needed more of the truth to build the life skills that would help me get through my own grief and understand what was happening, and how to cope with it all.

Love has a beautiful way of bringing people together. Sometimes even the most unsuspecting unions happen through fate. Loss and grief both have a very complex way of either strengthening these relationships or destroying them.

The people in our lives that have the biggest influence on us, shape who we become as we move through life. Some of the lessons that we consciously and subconsciously take with us form who we are at any given time. I have gone through years of transformations and some of the biggest ones have happened during important life events. I learned that before you can serve others, you have to serve yourself. It's so important to take care of *you* first, and then the other aspects of your life will be ok as well.

As a girl, I watched my grandmother and my mother do so much for others. They were my role models and I was always so inspired. They dedicated their lives to loving, caring for and serving others. They lived so selflessly; it was something I admired. Being one of the people who they showed such unconditional love to made me aspire to be like that as well. I had so much love in me to give and to share. Now, with both no longer here, it would be a shame not to be able to carry on their legacy of love and selflessness.

This is where the courage to change after experiencing loss begins for me. Perhaps these changes were a long time coming regardless of loss in life, but nevertheless it has been a tough journey to get here. We are the sum of our experiences, and at this point in my life I am ready to receive and embrace change.

Change is inevitable. If we choose to live with the idea of impermanence, then change doesn't have to be seen in a negative context at all. Change can actually be beautiful. How much more precious does the world seem when you've experienced loss? Break through the ideals that all will be well, and rather be present to the idea you may not always have the happy ending you wished for; but that is ok.

That knowledge makes you even more present to what you have in the *now*. By becoming more present to that, life has taken on a whole new meaning for me.

Adapting to the ever-changing space around me took courage, strength and sometimes blind faith. There were some significant areas of change that had to begin within me in order to make this transition transformational. Who knew these life lessons had always been right under my nose? Lessons that both those lovely souls; my mother and grandmother, had learned as well, and tried their best to live up to.

These transformational changes included reframing life events with perspective, making time for ME, and becoming present to the tangible idea that time is a commodity. Also, recognizing and reducing my stress load by managing the world around me and not letting the world manage me. Finally, recognizing that in a world of ideals and judgement, there is power in being vulnerable and embracing light through darkness.

Reframing life events with perspective sounds like one of the simplest concepts, yet when you are in the thick of loss or hurt or pain, it may not be that easy to accomplish. However, once I tried putting this into practice at work and in my home, I started thinking how much I could help myself heal by doing it for myself. By reframing something that has occurred that causes stress or pain or negativity, there is always another perspective that can be considered. Let's take the loss of my mother. Seemed so unfair, so hard to accept, she should have had more time with us etc. What if I try reframing that extremely tough situation? Not trivialize or minimize those genuine feelings, but rather take a stab at it from another perspective. What I feel is real however, with reframing I can imagine if it was me that had gotten sick and died instead of her. I can imagine her living with the loss of me and the pain that she would have endured. Would she have had the coping skills to carry on living well? Or would I want to be the one to endure that pain instead?

The beauty of taking this step back and reframing the big picture puts your true feelings into perspective. It's a bit different than just saying, "Well, things could be worse". Reframing takes the actual event and responses to the event and works through an actual alternative but realistic perspective. Working through reframing within you is not as easy as it sounds. It can be much easier for someone other than you to look at your situation and offer an alternate perspective. Part of the courage to change without needing anyone else to do that for you is to be able to do it for yourself. Your reframe also becomes that much more valuable as only you know what 'could be worse'.

Practicing reframing in all aspects of my life, professionally and personally has had great impact on creating a path that leads to healing and adapting to new life normalities each day through change.

In early grief and loss, it's tough to gain or give perspective, much less even attempt to reframe. However the next area of change for me that I needed to explore was and still is the importance of making time for me. I remember once I became a mom, people saying don't forget to take time for yourself and self-care. I honestly used to also remember thinking...I'm a mom; the concept of taking time for myself sounds like a luxury never to be had again. Now in the throes of loss and grief, I wish more than ever I had put those practices into place back then, as it would now be second nature and a foundational strength that I could fall back on to ground my uneasy soul.

To get to reframing and perspective living, you need to know yourself and truly become aware of your inner needs, core values and true self. One of the only ways to accomplish this for me was finally, after all these years, deciding to stop and make time for myself and being present to my thoughts. For me, this meant being ok with being alone. In the silence, you are forced to face your thoughts and emotions. This can sound like a scary place to be. In fact, I feel my mother kept herself busy most of the time to avoid it, except on her walks. I remember her saying that going out for her walks alone and with nature meant she could think, laugh, cry, scream if needed, and nature was there to absorb it all. That time was just for her and I needed to find my time just for me.

Now, after practicing incorporating "me time", I fully understand how much this helps you live and live well. I am able to allow myself to be true to my thoughts and emotions and find ways to gain and reframe perspectives that also speak true to my heart. One of the toughest things is to make it a routine, however, you have to be better than your toughest excuse. Your health and wellness should be at the center of it all. I am the center of my own family and working on ensuring I am in a good place can and will only benefit those around me that I love. Take time for you, know what it is you need, truly need and be present to practice day by day- bit by bit- to put it all back together again. You will be happy you took the time to do so.

Time has always been a source of anxiety. When I was younger, I couldn't wait for time to speed up so I could be older and independent. I can think of so many other times too where I couldn't wait for things to hurry up and happen. Once I became a mother, time had a whole new meaning for me. I remember the moment I almost lost my own life when I gave birth to my first-born. Handing him over to my husband because I didn't have enough strength to hold him as life was leaving my body. I also remember looking over at them both and thinking: *NO, this can't be my time.* In that moment, time stood still and I decided that I didn't come this far in life for it to end there. Barely having a pulse, I knew I needed to better negotiate for each day going forward. As my kids have grown so fast, and as much as I want to see them experience life and grow and learn, I also secretly wish that time would slow down. I want to take my time cherishing each and every moment we have together. Time and I stopped negotiating, but now there is an anxiety that comes from wondering what happens if there was no more time. What if something were to happen that took time away from this beautiful life and what I want to experience with them? I ended up being at the mercy of time. I decided to take a leap of faith and try to take time into my own hands.

I decided that after 16 years at a corporate job working for others, that I would become self-employed. This would not only allow me more time for myself and my family, but also more time with my retired mom. The time we never really had growing up as she worked at her career 5am to 7pm and then as a wife, mom and sister taking care of everyone else around her. But time had other plans for us, and presented us with the unexpected and sudden monster called cancer. Time was up. It made me do a deep dive into despair, self-pity and the feeling of defeat. So how do I move on from there? How do I reframe and gain perspective? I become present to the tangible idea that time is a commodity.

Time moves and either I become in tune with its movement or get left behind. Time lives and breathes with me, whether people around me are attuning to this same feeling about time or not. I cannot allow it to stop me. I need to keep on moving with its flow, good and bad and everything in between. Instead of living in anger and regret, I choose to see time almost as a child again; in a hurry to live the happy days in life when we make plans for the future. Instead of living in the past, I think of each day as a blessing and opportunity to live and be better than our yesterdays. Make the moments that you wish to have in the future, your realities *today*. In the end, todays are all we have.

So how do I take advantage of the time I have here to spend and share? By managing the world around me and not allowing the world to manage me. This sounds simple, but until you realize this is happening it is extremely difficult to identify, understand and make a change. Ever have those days where you feel that you're working constantly and then find out that you did not gain any ground or accomplish what you set out to originally do? Or those times where you feel the weight of the world on your shoulders and not quite sure why? Well through the process of losing my mother, there was a tremendous amount of that for me. In the aftermath of all this, I learned another very important lesson and that was how to deal with the external stressors that I have allowed to manage my life. These may be people around me or circumstances that appear to be priority based on how they present themselves. These seem so important, but are they? Being able to recognize when this is happening is not always easy. Learning to stop, step back, assess the situation and determine the priorities in life has made a huge difference. Of the billions of people on this earth, I am blessed with this family. They are and will always be my priority and I can only hope they carry the same core values throughout their lives when I too pass on.

This leads me to my final transitional change through this journey of love and loss. This is the power of change through being vulnerable and true. At my mother's funeral, I delivered the eulogy. Looking back, I'm not sure how I was able to stand and face everyone in that crowd of people; when the only person I wanted to be with wasn't there, my mother. I began writing that eulogy at 1am the morning of the funeral and finished the last sentence as we pulled into the parking lot. That morning, the image of the lotus flower was sent to me. How fitting to describe my mother's life and her soul.

The lotus perfectly represents the power to be vulnerable in a world of uncertainty. The power to overcome adversity and find light and beauty through darkness. The lotus is noted for the way that it grows. Before it can blossom in the sun, it must make its way through muddy waters and muck. In time, the lotus rises above the water and emerges beautiful and whole. The lesson the lotus brings is that we must honour the darkest parts of ourselves and the most painful of our life's experiences. It is those life moments that allow us to birth our most beautiful self. It is through the generations of people I love and have lost and this beautiful reminder sent from my mother, that I pay respect.

Knowing how much seems to be against the odds or how much has changed around me, or how many more people living that I will lose, I will choose the path of my true self and vulnerability. I will be present to the law of impermanence and be grateful for time. Everything changes, every day. To endure pain only means we have loved. Trust the process. There is a purpose to everything happening. I stood up there at the funeral giving her eulogy and felt honoured that I could depict her life so well. Yet that gift of being true, genuine, honest and vulnerable has provided me with strength to be able to stand up again and again in the face of adversity and have the courage to just be me. I will live for today and give thanks to everything that has made up my past, stay true to the present and the life I live, today, tomorrow and always.

HEALING
FROM WITHIN

The Courage to Change

Tracy Turberfield

Tracy is an International Luxury Travel Specialist whose passion is to *Co-Create Extraordinary Vacation Experiences* for her clients. Having held positions onboard a variety of cruise ships for many years as Head of the Guest Relations, and working in a travel agency as top consultant for 10 years; Tracy's passion and drive led her to taking the leap of faith into Entrepreneurship and creating her own travel business and brand, JUST GO Luxury Travel Experiences.

As a newly single mom she has been on a journey of life lessons, self-discovery, and deep healing. Her daughter Brooklynn is the light of her life and it was when she became a mom herself that she realized the importance of healing the parts of her own childhood that were holding her back from being the amazing woman and mother she was meant to be.

She hopes that her story will touch the hearts and souls of others so they may recognize the power within themselves and choose a life full of love and joy.

Healing Through Forgiveness
by Tracy Turberfield

I remember the footsteps and the sound of the stall doors opening and closing on either side of me, the toilets flushing and the tap water running. As the giggles of the girls filled the air, I tried not to breathe too heavy or move too much behind the door of the bathroom stall where I was hiding. Just a couple more seconds and they would be gone and I could undo my Saran-wrapped sandwich and eat it quickly. No one would know. I wouldn't have to walk in the cafeteria again and look desperately around for a seat that wasn't too close to anyone else so I didn't have to try to pretend that I fit in. If I eat my lunch in the bathroom stall again, I could just be invisible, truly invisible. And that was much better than feeling invisible in a giant cafeteria filled with high school students having fun with their friends.

I gulped down the last bite just as another round of girls came running in. I waited until I heard their doors lock then I flushed the toilet just to pretend, unlatched the door, and went out to the sink. One of the girls came out quite quickly and stood beside me at the counter. There we were, just two girls washing our hands. No one would ever guess the real reason I was in the bathroom.

High school was actually better than my earlier school years. I had a wonderful teacher, Ms. Cook, who took me under her wing and was the one person at school that I didn't feel invisible with. And, I had a crush on a boy. It was one-sided, but I remember being so in awe of him and drooling over his every word. He had long, blonde hair and was the coolest guy I had ever met. We had become friends and even worked together, all the while my heart beating out of my chest whenever I was near him. But it was not just these two people that made high school a bit better. It was the fact that, finally, after so many years of being afraid to step outside school at the end of the day, I didn't have a bully waiting on the other side of the doors to scare me and taunt me like I had in elementary and middle school. In grade 7 her name was Fara. We had moved unexpectedly from Toronto to the small town of Lindsay in the middle of the school year, where I didn't know a soul. It was scary. I was used to not fitting in and feeling alone and I subconsciously carried these feelings and beliefs with me through this transition.

It didn't take long before Fara picked up on this weakness. I was like a glow stick waving in the dark for her. She would wait for me at break times and after school. Her verbal lashings of how stupid and ugly I was cut me deep. Sometimes, I stayed after school with my teachers asking to help them with anything to prolong going outside to walk home. I never knew if she would be out there waiting for me. But when she was, she followed me and taunted me, sometimes nudging or pushing me over on the sidewalk. This bullying had become expected and I had become accustomed to it. I was nobody anyway, just like I had been in elementary school.

In Grade 4, her name was Leanne. I will always remember her name. It has been engraved in my memory and my wounds. We had all been friends, a group of us, but then something changed, I don't even recall what, and suddenly it was them against me. I don't know what was worse- the physical bullying or the taunting, but they both made me feel worthless. I remember one particular morning like it was yesterday.

I was walking to school when I noticed that Leanne and her friends were following me. They were laughing and taunting as usual, but that day they started threatening me too. Her words were very clear: "I'm going to get you after school .I'm going to punch you in your braces." I was scared the whole day. My tummy was upset. I felt sick. I felt alone and invisible.

True to her threat, Leanne was waiting for me on the sidewalk outside the school that afternoon. I tried to ignore her and kept walking, but the taunting turned to pushing and blocking my path. "I'm going to punch you in your braces," she kept saying. And then she did. I fell to the ground and could hear the kids laughing at me while they walked away and left me there. I wiped the tears that were streaming down my face, my eyes burning and the humiliation stinging my soul. At the time, I didn't know why I hadn't fought back.

As an adult in my mid-40s writing this now, I do know why. I was a scared little girl who could not understand the world around her. I learned later in my life that bullies gravitate to the weak, because it makes them feel strong. I can see why I was her target. I was just a 9-year-old kid with no confidence and no presence, who felt sad and alone all the time at school and at home.

My mom was a single parent raising me and my sister by herself. It was more than she could handle and alcohol was her best friend. It numbed her, I suppose. It let her escape her own loneliness and all the pressures of working several jobs, the bill collectors, the responsibilities of motherhood, the constant fight to stay above water. I remember hearing her cry behind her bedroom door. I can still see that exhausted and desperate look in her eyes. She was a fighter. But it looked like she was always fighting for her life.

Late at night, when I knew it was way past my bedtime, I would stay up watching TV so the silence of the apartment wouldn't swallow me whole. There it would be flashing on the screen, the Channel 7 News, "It's 11 o'clock; do you know where your children are?" I would think to myself that I didn't know where my mommy was. She was often in bars at that time of night, and I would call my grandmother after it got dark outside. She would keep me company on the phone.

My grandmother was my angel in life and in death. She was my safe place, and my fondest childhood memories are of being with her in her little apartment and watching *The Young and the Restless* together. She taught me how to make the best cup of orange pekoe tea and this was our "thing." I still drink tea every single day, it is my subconscious connection to her. When I slept over, we each had a single bed in her room, and she taught me how to make my bed, tucking in all the corners straight; a lesson I pass on to my own nine year-old daughter now.

I had another angel on earth. Her name is Lorrie Ann and we were best friends in fourth and fifth grade. At the time, I didn't know how important her presence in my life really was. But looking back, she too was a safe place from the storm and isolation.

It is truly amazing how the universe works and brings us the gifts we need in divine timing. Lorrie Ann and I had lost touch for three decades and unexpectedly reconnected in our mid-forties when her sister recognized me through social media. We squealed like children again over Facebook messenger, reminiscing about our time together when we were little girls. My childhood memories had been buried so deep that it took Lorrie Ann recounting them to me in detail to unlock them and remind me of the fun times we had together despite the darkness I lived in.

We were snarky and bad sometimes, like when we dressed up and would go around our apartment building doing door to door canvassing for fake campaigns because we wanted money for candy. We were only nine years old! Today, I spearhead many charitable events with all the money going directly to the cause!

Lorrie Ann also reminded me of the time my mom made a turkey and left the carcass sitting in the oven all weekend. We came home from school on Monday to a horrendous, foul smell and followed the scent to the oven. We took the whole roasting pan down the hall to the incinerator and dumped it in, hearing it bang and crash several floors down to the bottom. No one ever even questioned where that turkey and roasting pan went!

Lorrie Ann's friendship was my escape, and she knew my mom was on her own journey. I spent three decades having this one particular vision in my mind of seeing my mom slumped over and passed out in the back of a car that was driving down into the underground parking of our apartment. I felt helpless and sad seeing my mom in this state, not knowing how to help her. Through the years, I could never figure out if this vision was real as it seemed so distant and blurry, yet it caused such a deep sadness in my heart. I recounted this vision several times in therapy and counselling sessions in my twenties and thirties. It was always exactly the same.

It wasn't until Lorrie Ann and I reconnected over 30 years later that it was made clear. We were taking a trip down memory lane and she brought up that event. She recounted it exactly as I had seen it in my mind and felt it for all those years. I burst into tears at the validation of this memory. Lorrie Ann was my rock back then and her perspective in adulthood now has been very healing for me.

"She definitely taught you a lot ... and prepared you for life...look at yourself!! You're fabulous.... we all grew up in different situations but we survived and we learned sometimes the hard way."

Reading those words brought tears to my eyes as I sat in clarity of how far I had come since being that scared and lonely little girl. I basked in gratitude for the journey I had been on for the three years leading up to telling this story, being so thankful for the understanding, healing, and forgiveness. Looking back, I now realize that I spent decades marinating in anger and resentment for everything I thought my mother was not.

She had boyfriends, lots of them, most of them married. I would watch her crying over them as they would leave our house to go back to their own. She was chasing love. But at the time I didn't know why. I didn't know that when my sister and I were kids that my mom was raped by one of her boyfriends and told not to scream or he would go after her little girls asleep in the next room. I didn't know then that I was not her first-born child, and that she had gotten pregnant in her early twenties. She had been raised to believe that being pregnant out of wedlock was a sin. Her father banished her and forced her to give up her baby boy three days after she gave birth. She never saw him again. I didn't know she had that gaping hole in her heart, carrying that pain with her every day. I assumed that she preferred alcohol and men over me. I didn't know she was chasing love and trying desperately to fill a void. All I saw and felt was a mommy who wasn't giving me the love I so desperately wanted.

At 16, I immediately bought a car and, within a few months, packed up my room in our house, and moved out. I couldn't pack my car fast enough. It was a desperation so deep that it felt like I was drowning in the sea. Moving out of that house that day was my life raft. I knew it was breaking her heart and the guilt of that ate at me, but I had to go. The choice was clear; it was reclaiming my life or a slow, painful death.

My sadness and anger were burrowed so deep inside my cells, much deeper than I even knew. I spent the next ten years living in various apartments and attending university and college. I had heartbreaks and I broke some hearts. During this time, my resentment towards my mother continued because she was forever struggling to make ends meet and often needed help to pay her bills and buy groceries. Regularly, I would begrudgingly give her money, buy her groceries, and pay her utility bills as she was continuing to fight for her life just as she did when I was a child. That look of exhaustion and desperation in her eyes was constantly there. I teeter-tottered between empathy for her on my good days and anger and hatred on my bad days. Then on June18, 2008, my mom called me with the worst news I could ever have imagined. My grandmother had died in her sleep.

My heart broke into a zillion pieces right then and there. I fell to the ground, dropping the phone. My safe place was shattered and I was truly alone, more alone than I ever knew I could be. It was so dark, and got darker still when I learned that my mom had decided to use my grandmother's small amount of life insurance money to pay her own bills and buy a small, used car instead of paying for the funeral expenses. This news threw me into a rage, and I wrote her off right then and there. I didn't care that my mom had not a cent to her name, that she needed a vehicle of some kind to get around, that her utilities were about to be shut off, and her fridge was empty again.

This was her story, her pattern, and I hated it. I was blinded by what I saw, what I thought I knew. I didn't know then that swimming in this negativity was eating me up from the inside out.

I hated it. I hated it so much until another phone call just over a year later on Jan 5, 2009 at one in the morning, five weeks before my wedding. It was my sister, frantic, saying words that I could barely digest. Our mom had had a heart attack and a stroke and was being airlifted to hospital. I couldn't breathe, I couldn't think, I couldn't do anything except beg God to not let her die. For the next seven days, as I watched her lying in that hospital bed with tubes and machines keeping her barely alive, I begged. I pleaded. I prayed. She was in a coma with no brain activity. She lay perfectly still. I would have given anything to see her fingers move or her eyelids flutter. I sat there beside her day and night holding her hand in mine and bargaining with her to wake up.

If you wake up we can do this, we will go here together and do that together. But she didn't wake up and the doctors finally told us the words we dreaded to hear. She wasn't going to wake up, ever, and it was time to let her go.

We all stood around her closely and as the nurse took out the breathing tube the noise I heard next will stain my ears forever. It was my own voice, my piercing shriek bellowing out from some place deep inside my core, as my mom gasped her own last breath and the lines on the machines went flat. There are no words I can share to adequately describe the feeling of sheer emptiness. She was gone. This woman I spent my whole life hating for not being who I needed her to be, and now I would give anything, *anything*, to have her wake up.

Three days later was the Jack and Jill for my wedding that had been planned for months. It was also the day we buried my mother. After the funeral church service, we were all standing outside at the cemetery on that bitter cold January day as I watched that casket being laid into the ground. I kept thinking that this couldn't really be happening. How were we supposed to make amends? How were we supposed to make up? What was I supposed to do with my 30 years of anger, resentment, sadness and desperation for love? Where was I supposed to put it all now? How was I supposed to try to understand now? I know I was living in loathing for so long but it wasn't supposed to be this way. She wasn't supposed to leave me, not again. She had left me so many times before, when all I truly wanted was to be snuggled up on her lap and loved. And now she had left me again, forever. How was I supposed to tell her I love her? She was gone and I was alone again.

I didn't know any of the answers. What I knew was that my wedding was in four weeks and this heartache was too much to bear. We were getting married in Mexico with just a small group of friends. But now it didn't seem right at all to have this wedding without my mom somehow being there. I noticed that I had not been concerned about that before, but now it was everything to me. So, in three weeks we threw together a church wedding. It was the church I grew up going to, the one my grandmother's funeral was in, the same one I had just watched my mother's coffin be carried through the aisles of three weeks before. It seemed only fitting that I got married where they had last been.

My new life was starting and my heart was broken. I did all I knew how to do; hang on tight to the part of my heart that had been frozen for so long and keep moving. It was safer there. Or so I thought. I didn't know that those two losses were the start of the rollercoaster of losses and an incredible life-changing journey. The next few years brought different heartaches with the loss of my uncle to cancer, my own cervical cancer scare, and losing two more babies, both in the 1st trimester of my pregnancies. (I had lost one as well before I met my husband). But in amongst all these losses, an incredible, amazing gift was given to me that changed everything. The birth of my healthy, sweet baby doll, my beautiful daughter Brooklynn Maia. From the moment I peed on that stick and it turned positive, I knew she was going to be the light in my life and my guiding compass. Little did I know, however, just how true that was. One thing I knew for sure was that my number one priority was that my daughter would be embraced in unlimited love and affection. Alcohol was never going to be a part of our lives. I am so thankful that it never has been.

Life got busy as it tends to do and we had struggles that were very familiar to me in other ways. Financial struggles, always trying to make ends meet, this is what I knew. I recognized this. And we had struggles in our marriage that caused stress and often emotional pain and mental anguish. As I was navigating motherhood, a rocky marriage and a full-time career, I was on autopilot and soon burnt out. I found myself struggling to feel anything but sadness and heartache. But I was a fighter, like my mom, and I was determined to keep the Pandora's box that housed all the grief and memories of my childhood and my mother's death, closed. Little did I know that opening that Pandora 's box was the key to the magnificent lessons I was about to learn.

On the way to my job one morning, I could feel the anxiety building as I got each kilometre closer to my workplace. It was a familiar feeling with my palms starting to sweat and my heart racing, but this time, it felt like a ton of bricks had dropped on my chest and I couldn't breathe. I was in a full-blown panic and had to pull over to the side of the road on the highway. It felt like every ounce of pain, every memory, every lonely moment, every tear, every loss and every heartache I had ever experienced since I was a toddler; was falling like concrete slabs and pummelling my heart. I was completely and utterly lost, like a scared child who wanted to be found.

That was the last day I drove to that job, and it was the beginning of the journey to healing the broken little girl inside me who was walking around in an adult woman's body, desperate to be seen and loved. The lesson I learned over the next 3 years was bigger and more life-changing than I could ever have imagined.

Like my mom, I spent my whole life looking for love outside myself, when the entire time I was carrying the answer within me every single day and couldn't see it.

The answer was ME. The person I wanted love from, and needed love from the most was myself. The person I needed to help me heal was me. As the saying goes "you don't know what you don't know." I didn't know, and it is by the grace of this beautiful universe and the earth angels who crossed my path, that I was blessed with the lessons that started to unfold on my journey to self-discovery.

I remember the first time I met her. I had decided to attend a workshop that was way out of my comfort zone. As we all sat in that room and listened to the voice of the woman facilitating, I was taken on a journey. I walked down a path towards a big beautiful meadow filled with trees and flowers. In the distance, just over the hill, I saw the silhouette of a little child- a girl with long curly brown hair. She looked about four years old. My heart leaped and I started to walk faster toward her. She saw me then and started to run, her smile widening and her excitement visible. I started to run. It was my daughter, Brooklynn. But as I got closer I suddenly realized it wasn't. That little girl running with all her might towards me was *me*. We ran faster and faster across the meadow and when we reached each other, she jumped up into my arms and squeezed me so tight wrapping her arms around me for dear life. I felt my tears spilling down my cheeks and heard myself saying, "I love you, I love you, I love you."

We sat together in the grass under a beautiful apple tree and she snuggled in my lap. We talked and she told me she missed me and loved me. I told her how happy I was to find her again and that I was so sorry for abandoning her, and I would never ever leave her again. I told her she was safe and protected, and that I would always take care of her. She was so happy as she hugged me and looked up at me with a new awareness in her eyes. After sitting together holding each other and feeling this beautiful love between us, we got up from the grass and looked into each other's eyes. I cupped her cheeks in my hands and told her that I would always be with her and that she could go back over the hill into the meadow and play; we would be together in our hearts forever. I told her that anytime she wants to talk to me or see me, all she has to do is reach into her heart and I am there. She was very content and safe in this knowledge and slowly turned to the hill and skipped toward it, looking back with a smile. As I came back into my body from that subconscious state and breathed deeply, opening my eyes slowly, I knew my life was changed. I felt different. I felt lighter. I felt loved. I felt found.

From that day onwards, my heart was open. I was ready to receive, to learn, to heal, and most importantly to forgive. People started coming into my life; the type of people I had never known before. They had this aura around them, this welcoming, this light that shone so bright like I had never seen before. I started hearing their stories, and absorbing the lessons they were teaching through their triumph over tragedy and heartache. There is a common bond between people who share their vulnerability and truly expose their authentic selves, and I was very slowly listening with my ears and my heart.

I had never talked about my mom, not anything good at least. It was always bitter words and sad stories if I referred to her. Slowly, I began to see her through a different lens. When I thought of her, I could feel the ice melting a little bit each time. I was thinking of her with my heart now because my heart was open and I had made space for more than resentment, anger and hostility. I had made space for clarity, perspective, and for forgiveness.

I had always thought that I could never forgive my mom, because that would mean to me that I was letting her off the hook for all my pain and suffering. But now I felt different. I was learning, in baby steps, that forgiving her came from allowing myself the permission to see the story through a different lens; one that was clear, unfiltered and cleansed of all those negative emotions and feelings I had been carrying for decades. It took a lot, a whole lot, of working through the memories, sitting with them, allowing myself to remember and not shut down. Now I was choosing to see the whole picture not just my version. Now I was allowing myself to understand and accept that she did the best she could with the tools she had. Now I was seeing her struggles, understanding her traumas, and how they had such a ripple effect on her own feelings and relationship with her own little four-year-old self, teenage self, and young adult self. I will never know if she ever met them, but what I do know is that meeting my own inner child and creating that reconnection and loving bond between us; allowed me to open my heart and allow healing and love to live there now. This was the gateway to the Pandora's box that not only held all the childhood memories, but also the key to so much healing. And, it paved the path to forgiving my mom and setting us both free.

As I write this, I know wholeheartedly that she is up in heaven watching over me and my daughter, and loving us deeply with all the love she could never find a way to express on earth. It is because of her that I can teach my daughter the profound power of forgiveness, and for that I am forever grateful.

I love you mom.

Angela Brown

Angela Brown, a Financial Advisor. On December 16, 2012, after attending a business event, someone T-boned her car. The accident may only have lasted thirty seconds, but it totally changed her life forever. Angela said, "I endured many months of pain and agony, been told that I have whiplash and it would get better with time." With surgery and physiotherapy and other therapies, the bad news was that her previous profession as an Early Childhood Educator was no longer an option. At this point her neck is 95% fused and any further injury could mean being paralyzed or dead.

Even though she still suffers from pain and symptoms from Post Traumatic Stress Disorder, Angela gets out of bed each day with the focus to help others.

Angela's business is focused on helping her clients prepare for the unexpected. What if they had an accident like hers – where would the money come from while going through therapy?

Every day, Angela tries her best to "live for today". Her business helps her clients "live for today" without the worry about tomorrow.

Miracle of God
by Angela Brown

Many doctors, nurses, medical technicians, have told me repeatedly that I'm a medical miracle, I'm special, or rare. They look at me with excitement, expecting me to be excited too. But I've never felt like a medical miracle, until December 16, 2012. That night an incident that may have lasted thirty seconds changed my opinion and my life forever.

My journey began on July 16, 1964, in Huddersfield, UK, where I was born. I had one sister, Suzette, who was one year older than me. I was born premature with several congenital abnormalities and heart disease. I became a patient from that day on. And, as I grew up, doctors realized that my health issues were more severe than initially thought.

When I was two years old, my mother left my father in the United Kingdom and moved to Jamaica with Suzette and me. She later left Jamaica, leaving Suzette and me behind with my grandmother. I loved living in Jamaica. It was hot most days, and I liked the feeling of the warm sun on my face. I loved the fruits, especially the star apples, June plums, soursops, the sweetness of oranges, mangoes, and sugar cane.

Every Sunday morning, we woke up to my grandmother playing and singing gospel music. She would give us a bible study class, and we had to recite a psalm and then she would give us another one to memorize for the next week. Then we would go to church for a few hours.

Whenever I got sick, my grandmother would take me to the hospital where the doctor would give me an injection of antibiotics. As I grew up, this became a regular routine, because she was worried that I would get worse. Sometimes I tried to hide from her when I wasn't feeling well, but she always knew, so we would go to the hospital.

On February 28, 1973, at eight years old, Suzette and I left Jamaica and went to Canada to live with our mom. We left our "mamma" and moved to a strange country to live with someone we barely knew. We had seen her pictures, and she sent gifts for us. She would visit for a short time, and we were always sad to see her go.

We were warned that it would be cold, but nothing could prepare us for the experience. My mom gave us sweaters, coats, hats, gloves, scarves, and boots to put on. But even with all we had to wear, it was still freezing. So cold that there was steam coming from our noses and mouths. I was happy to see my mom, but I was scared too. I couldn't stop looking at her face to see if it was real or a dream. The best part of the reunion was being met by baby sister Kareena who was two years old. I always wanted to be a big sister; it felt great!

We began school, which I immediately hated. I was called names and bullied almost every day. I was a prime target for bullies because of my small stature. Being shy and introverted, I was always picked on, hit, and ridiculed. I thought since I was in a new country, maybe it would be different, but it was much worse. I was called names like dwarf, shrimp, midget, and worst of all, nigger. This was my first introduction to racism.

My grandmother told my mom that I was sick a lot. I was eight years old and weighed only thirty-eight pounds at three feet, six inches tall. Clearly, I was very underdeveloped for my age. The doctors said I needed surgery that could not be performed in Jamaica. They did not have the medical knowledge and equipment necessary to do the surgery. A few weeks after we came to Canada, my mom took me to The Hospital for Sick Children. The doctors told her that I had two holes in my heart along with valve malformation, a groin hernia and scoliosis, which was a curved spine, and strabismus in my right eye.

The doctors said I would need surgery as soon as possible. They would have to perform two to three operations to repair my heart and valve. My mom was also told that if I had remained in Jamaica for an additional six months, I would be dead. Suzette once told me a story about the two of us going to the mall. A lady stopped us and gave her money, telling her to buy me some food. My sister tried to explain that I was sick, but the lady insisted she take the money.

When surgery day came, I was so scared, and I knew my mom was scared too. She told me it was an eight-hour surgery. She prayed the whole time that I would be okay. My surgery was performed by a famous cardiac surgeon, Dr. Mustard, at the Hospital for Sick Children, one year before he retired. I was in the hospital for two months. So that I didn't fall behind at school, Suzette would bring me homework from my teacher. The hospital had a room set up with a teacher to help us. I received very nice cards from my teacher and classmates. I also received other gifts like the furry, purple winter coat from my mom's co-workers, and my favourite, the doll from my mother. Mrs. Beasley came from my favourite TV show, Family Affair. I really loved her- she was my best friend, and I told her all my secrets.

I made friends with the nurses, doctors, and other children. When I was feeling up to it, I would go to the playroom and play games with the other kids; my favourite was Trouble. Since there were four kids in a room, there was always someone to play or talk to if we felt like it. Sometimes I just played with Mrs. Beasley or other stuffed animals. We had two TVs in our room, one on each side to share and it was attached from the ceiling. We had to ask the nurses to turn it off and on, and we all had to watch the same thing. Otherwise, it would be too distracting. We had a lot of fun and laughed with each other.

My mom was not able to visit every day. She had to work and take care of Suzette and Kareena. It was the same for some of the other kid's parents. So, we had to make the best of the situation. We didn't have phones in our rooms so, when my mom called, I would have to go to the nurse's desk to talk to her and not for a long time. She just wanted to check in to see how I was doing. If I was unable to go to the desk, the nurses would tell me that she called and she said, "I love you, and I will visit soon!" It usually worked out that at least one parent would visit, so they became the substitute parent for all the kids in the room.

When I returned to school, I was not allowed to go outside for recess. I stayed in the library, helped the librarian, and read a lot. I decided to become a librarian when I grew up. When my classmates were going to swim class or going on class field trips, I still was not allowed to go. Of course, it made me more of an outcast, and I still had no friends.

At home, when I couldn't go to school, I played 'school'; I would line up my dolls and stuffed animals across my bed and gave them names. Then I would teach them and talk with them as if they were real. Sometimes, if she would let me, I would use Kareena as my human pupil. When someone asked, "What do you want to be when you grow up?" I would say "a teacher or a librarian."

After my second surgery when I returned from Christmas break, I got a big surprise. My teacher gave me a box wrapped with Christmas paper. I was so excited to open it. Inside was a lemon-scented perfume from a classmate. I never used the perfume, but I kept it for a long time as a reminder that they thought of me.

In later school years, I made some friends. It was nice to hang out with them on weekends, and during the Christmas and summer breaks. It was hard for me to get close to them because our lives were so different. I never invited them to my house because it just wasn't something we did in my family. They did invite me to their homes. I met their parents and siblings, and they treated me like a part of their family. When I graduated high school, my whole family came, and I introduced them to my friends.

A few months before my eighteenth birthday, I had my last yearly check-up at the hospital for sick children. The doctors discovered a small pin hole in my heart, but surgery was not needed unless problems occurred in the future. I was warned by the cardiologist not to get pregnant because labour would be too hard for my heart.

I had my first boyfriend at age 18; my mom had set up a meeting with one of her young co-workers. He was very friendly, and we had a lot of fun together. We dated off and on for six years. My family loved him and thought he was a good match for me. They all saw marriage in our future, including him. But there was one problem, I just didn't see him as "the one." I didn't feel any butterflies when I saw him or any fireworks when he kissed me. I wanted the fairy-tale I read about in the Harlequin romance novels where we find our prince at the end.

On December 27,1989, I woke up feeling so excited I was going to start a new job. Then the telephone rang, and it was not good news. All excitement drained from my body when I heard my mom screaming. I rushed to her room and saw her crying uncontrollably. The person on the phone was my cousin in Jamaica. She said my grandmother had died the night before in her sleep. I was devastated; everyone was crying. I will never forget this date. The next few days everyone was going on autopilot. There were lots of tears and laughter as we remembered stories about my grandmother. My mom and Suzette went to Jamaica for the funeral. I was very disappointed that I couldn't go too, but I just started a new job so I couldn't get the time off.

A few months later, I was diagnosed with a huge uterine fibroid which meant another surgery to remove it. The fibroid was attached to the outside of my uterus, so the doctor suggested that I have a hysterectomy. I was twenty-six years old and never had any children. I didn't want to risk the chance of never having a child. The doctor agreed not to do a hysterectomy unless there were any complications. I received a miracle from God, everything went well; I did not have a hysterectomy.

In the summer of 1991, my best friend Ivita and I went to Jamaica on vacation to visit my parents, who had retired early to handle my grandmother's business and estate. While we were there, my mother connected me with someone I knew when I was younger. He became one of our tour guides for the remainder of our vacation. When I returned to Canada, we started writing letters to each other. Six months later, he came to Canada, and we were married on May 30, 1992.

Soon after I got married, I wanted to have a baby. We went to see a Cardiologist because it had been ten years since I was warned not to get pregnant. After a few tests, he said I could have one or two babies, but I would have to deliver by caesarean section. Six months after getting married, I became pregnant, but I had a miscarriage shortly after. We were very disappointed, but six weeks after the miscarriage we decided to try again. A few weeks later I was pregnant. We were all so excited and couldn't wait for the baby to come.

My pregnancy was very tense, everyone was worried about heart complications during delivery. I had doctors' appointments every week. I had between four to six ultrasounds. I had problems gaining weight, and I vomited after every meal. Eventually, I only ate soup and porridge-that's all my stomach could tolerate. I gained eleven pounds throughout my pregnancy and gave birth at thirty-eight weeks.

On August 26, 1993, I gave birth to my miracle baby girl by caesarean section. Natasha Justine Brown weighed five pounds nine ounces. She was completely healthy and showed no signs of congenital heart disease. When I saw her, I was so happy. I had done what many doctors had thought was impossible. After four hours, a nurse woke me up to feed her. I looked at my beautiful daughter and felt so much love that I'd never felt before. The pregnancy had not gone as smoothly as I thought, but it was all worth it to have my miracle baby daughter.

In 1998 I began to have problems turning my neck for hours, sometimes days. I was in extreme pain. I had numbness and tingling in both hands and a feeling like electrical shocks in my body. It became so severe that I was having problems doing ordinary things like writing, washing dishes, laundry, typing- all which meant I couldn't work. My doctor referred me to a Neurologist, and I was put on a waiting list to see her. Once I saw the Neurologist, she ordered an MRI. The result was I had Short Neck Syndrome, which sounded very weird to me. She referred me to a neurosurgeon. He said I had several congenital spinal cord abnormalities, and I would need neck and back surgery.

I agreed to have neck surgery, even though it was a very risky surgery. The recovery doesn't always go as the doctors tell you. I still had some similar issues I had before surgery, and I had some new problems. Nine weeks after surgery, I returned to work but not for very long. Every day I came home in tears because of the pain. The only way to cope was by taking narcotic medication. Only my doctor knew how much I was taking. I was doing a good job at hiding my pain from everyone. I wanted to be a good wife, mother, and co-worker, but I felt like I was failing everyone.

For the next few years, it was a rollercoaster between work and being off. Finally, my doctor said I could no longer work. I was diagnosed with fibromyalgia, which caused me to have severe muscle pain, depression, insomnia, headaches, fatigue, mood changes, sleep apnea, restless legs, and tingling in my hands and feet.

My pain was taking over my whole life, which was taking a toll on my marriage. I hardly left my house or had visitors, and my husband was rarely home. It became evident that my husband and I were living two different lives, like two ships sailing in different directions. I decided to try counselling, but he refused to go with me. Eventually, I stopped going because I realized it was impossible to fix our marriage by myself. In June of 2001, my husband and I separated, and six years later, we were divorced.

Then everything changed on December 16, 2012.

It was around 9:00 pm. It was a clear dry night and very mild. I was dropping someone home from a business event we had both attended. As I entered the intersection, I saw a vehicle coming from the opposite direction. She did not have her indicators on and so, I assumed the car was going straight. As we proceeded through the intersection, she began to make a left turn without stopping.

Then she hit my car. It went spinning around twice and then smashed into the traffic post. The accident may only have lasted thirty seconds, but it totally changed my life forever. The paramedics put a neck brace on me, took me out of the car, strapped me onto a backboard, and put me in the ambulance. It was like a movie. I was finally able to call Natasha and told her to meet me at the hospital. Once we arrived at the hospital, I was put in a waiting area in the hallway for what seemed like hours. I was having a lot of pain. The back brace was uncomfortable, and the neck brace was very tight.

Natasha finally came and I was so happy to see her. I could see she was distraught and had been crying. I told her I was in a lot of pain and was feeling nauseous, so she ran to get a nurse. A while later, I was taken to get an x-ray of my neck. Around 1:00 am, the doctor came, and he told us everything was fine. He took off the neck brace off and threw it into the trash can and told me I could leave. Natasha helped me get dressed, and she took the brace out of the garbage can. Natasha told me she had called Suzette, and she arrived around 2:00 am. Natasha suggested that I continue to wear the neck brace and I agreed. Suzette drove us home saying she would be back in a few hours.

A few weeks after my accident, I started physiotherapy. I was hoping this would help with the pain so I could get back to my normal life. Day after day, I went to physio and massage therapy, but the pain was more severe after every visit. I went home and crawled up in my bed and cried. The days turned into weeks and the weeks turned into months, but I was still suffering from headaches, sharp pain in the back of my head and ears, left shoulder pain, and it even hurt to chew. I also had some sensation of electrical pulses on my head.

My doctor referred me to a Neurologist after I told him about the electrical pulses in my head. A few days later, I saw the Neurologist, who requested I have an MRI. Three days after the MRI, the Neurologist called and told me I needed to go to the hospital as soon as possible because "my neck was not stable." She suggested taking an overnight bag. I called Natasha and told her what the Neurologist said, then she told me her dad would come and drive me to the hospital.

When I arrived at the hospital, I headed straight for the emergency department and gave them my name. As I waited, I replayed the phone conversation I had with the Neurologist. She had said, "your neck is not stable." I wondered what she meant. I waited for what seemed like an eternity, but it was only ten minutes. I was taken to a room with a bed, the nurse put a neck brace on me, she told me to lie down and don't go anywhere without asking first, not even to the bathroom.

About an hour later, the neurosurgeon came. He told me I had broken my neck and I needed surgery to repair the damage. He said it was a miracle that I survived for six months with this injury, I heard the same repeated from many doctors. I was told by one doctor, any wrong movement of my neck like going to the hairdresser could have been "lights out!" in his words. They couldn't believe I had been having physio and massage therapy for six months. My surgery was scheduled for the next morning, he explained the possible complications: becoming paralyzed, my voice could change, not being able to talk permanently, or death. I had to sign a waiver form that I understood the possible outcomes and consent to surgery. I tried not to think about the many things I had done over the last six months that could have been fatal. Natasha arrived a few hours later, and I told her about the surgery and the possible complications.

I didn't have surgery the next morning as originally planned. The neurosurgeon explained that I needed to be seen by a cardiologist to check my heart. I also needed to see an anaesthesiologist who could give permission for me to be put to sleep. In total, I saw four doctors outside of the neurology field. The surgery date kept changing because they were having problems organizing the surgery with four doctors from different areas being available on the same day and at the same time. Finally, the operation was scheduled for June 13, 2013, four days after I arrived at the hospital. I was terrified, but I knew that I needed to rely on God to get me through. I had many people at church pray for me and my recovery.

After the surgery, I was in an induced coma for two days. When I woke up, the neurosurgeon and a few interns and nurses were in the room. He explained that they were going to take out the tube, and I should not attempt to talk. He also explained that if I couldn't breathe on my own, they would immediately put the tube back in, which was very risky. I nodded that I understood. After the tube was taken out, I was unable to talk. I tried to write things down, but it looked like a toddler's scribbles. It was very frustrating not being able to communicate with people.

It took a few days for my voice and handwriting to get back to normal. I was wearing a neck brace, and I couldn't move my head and neck off the pillow at all; it felt so heavy and stiff. I was in the most excruciating pain that I've ever felt in my whole life; I thought I would die! I was sleeping a lot because of the pain medication, which was a blessing.

Every day, I had lots of visitors, sometimes there was a lineup because only two people could visit at the same time. One week after surgery, I received my custom-made body brace; it started at my chin to my belly button. It was very uncomfortable, itchy, and hot! I had to wear it every day except when having a shower; I had another brace for that. I was told I had to wear it for three months, and I was not looking forward to it.

After my custom-made brace arrived, I could feed myself. Then I was tested to see if I could chew solid food. I was so tired of pureed foods. Once the doctor was comfortable that I wouldn't choke, she gave permission for me to have some solid food. After three weeks in ICU, I was finally transferred to a regular room. A few days later, I was able to leave the hospital. I was so happy to be going home. I would have Personal Support Workers who came every day to help with my personal care. But I was told if things didn't work out at home, I would be going to a rehabilitation hospital for at least one month.

I had my first follow-up visit with the neurosurgeon six weeks after leaving the hospital. I was using a walker to help support my body. After an MRI, he told me everything was looking well, and he was so happy with my progress. He said I still had to wear the brace for another six weeks. I still need a PSW for personal care, range of motion exercises, daily walks, and light housekeeping.

I was counting down the days to my next appointment when I could take off the brace and be free to move around. My house was becoming like my prison since I couldn't go anywhere by myself. I would take short walks with the PSW but wearing the brace and using the walker made it very uncomfortable. Six weeks later, I saw the neurosurgeon again. I had a CT scan, then he told me everything was good, so I could take the brace off for one hour the next day and one additional hour every day until twenty-four days would be the last day. When the day came to take off the brace, it was the happiest day of this whole experience. I was now allowed to use a cane instead of a walker.

Two months later, I went back to see the neurosurgeon, without the walker or a cane. I had to do an x-ray before I saw the doctor. Once again, he said everything was going well, but he was surprised and concerned that I wasn't using a walker or a cane. I told him I felt stable and comfortable walking without them. He told me to be careful, and he would like me to use the walker a little longer. I continued to have six-month follow-ups with the neurosurgeon so he could evaluate my progress and any problems I was having.

The years have flown by since the surgery. I can no longer move my neck; it is 95% fused. The doctor told me to be especially careful because there's nothing left to fuse in my neck. Another neck injury would leave me paralyzed or dead. I suffer with pain everyday. I have tendinitis in both shoulders, tinnitus, daily headaches, sleep disturbances. It is tough to explain how this affects my everyday life. I lost my independence because I can no longer drive, and I'm terrified of taking public transit by myself. I must depend on others for a ride or take Uber. I try to hide how much pain I'm in as best I can, I don't want anyone feeling sorry for me or to ruin anyone's day!

I realize it is difficult for others to understand what it's like for people with Fibromyalgia, PTSD, chronic pain, chronic fatigue syndrome, and other chronic illnesses. I have tried physiotherapy, massage therapy, acupuncture, guided meditation, psychotherapy, Yoga, natural herbal treatments and medical cannabis as well. I now depend on prescribed medication to cope. I tried a few times to stop taking some of the medication cold turkey, but on one occasion, I ended up in the hospital.

I've been dealing with health issues my whole life. I'm so tired of being in pain, surgeries, needles, painful tests, being prodded and poked and the medications. I've learned to take things in stride, one day at a time because I don't know what tomorrow will bring. Being the sick one has held me back from many things and made me an outcast in school for many years. People didn't see Angela. I was invisible and hiding in the shadow of my sisters. Whenever I see someone I knew as a child, they don't even remember my name. I must identify myself as Suzette's sister or Josephine's daughter. Then they remember "the sickly one." There is no doubt that Suzette was much liked by everyone, she had no problems making friends. Kareena was bubbly, had a sweet innocent face and was always smiling, and Junior was the baby and the only boy in the family. Then there was me, the middle child. I was invisible, and had to "Yell" to be heard, and was described as skinny, boring, a nerd, or a bookworm.

I have learnt that I don't have to live my life based on how people see me or expect me to behave. My health doesn't have to define me, but it shapes who I am today. Because of my real-life experiences, I have become a strong, courageous, confident, intelligent and independent woman.

At 54 years old, I'm living my best life, partly due to a man named Kevin. I met him on a dating website in December 2017, and it has changed my life. He does not see me as sickly, dull, nerdy or flawed; he just sees me as me. We have gone on many adventures since we met. We took a road trip to Ottawa in August of 2018 and have attended several Raptors and Blue Jays games. He has become a significant part of my life, and I can see a long future for us.

It's been six years and three months since my accident. I feel better than I have in a long time. I'm healthy in my mind and body, I'm loved, and I have a great family and friends who provide excellent support when I need them.

I now have a career as a Financial Advisor for a large company. It is sometimes very challenging getting around because I can no longer drive, but I'm resilient and can handle any challenge. There are days when I have a lot of energy and can do anything, and other times, I can barely get out of bed. I've accepted that it's okay to have bad days when I don't feel "okay" I must accept the limitations of my body and not overdo it. I know that no matter what obstacles life throws at me, I can survive anything. I'm a survivor!

Barb Takeda

For many, many years Barbara showed up as not enough in her life; today she shows up as her perfectly imperfect Divine self. This Inspirational Speaker, Author, Reiki Master/Teacher, Mentor/Coach, and the creator of "An Exceptional Woman" event, is passionate about helping you cut through your limiting beliefs. She embraces being perfectly imperfect.

Living most of her life with debilitating chronic illness, depression and numerous losses; she found her light, which brought her through her dark night and into the light.

As she soul-searched through this dark period of her life, she came to understand that every step, every loss, every trauma, circumstance, and setback; was the Divine plan in action given for her soul's evolution and growth. She realized that all she had to do was be in full surrender and alignment; overcoming her victim mentality to become a victor. Whatever life throws her way, Barbara no longer questions "Why me", but responds with "Why not me?"

Barbara encourages and inspires women to unleash their greatness by giving them the practical spiritual principles and tools that she employed to help her find her way out of the darkness.

Coming Home
by Barb Takeda

She sat in the middle of the double bed she shared with her little sister, her tattered dress spread around her, silent tears tracing tracks down her cheeks. This time he had used the skipping rope. With each lash against her bare thighs she felt his fury, but then slowly tears formed at the corners of his eyes as he quietly spoke saying, "This hurts me too, but this is the only way you'll learn."

Her father was a practical joker, but also a stern disciplinarian who adhered religiously to the saying, "spare the rod, spoil the child", taken from the Biblical verse in Proverbs that says, "He who spares the rod hates his son, but he who loves him is careful to discipline him."

As she sat she wondered, what did she need to learn? At such a tender young age, she felt unworthy, unloved and certainly not good enough. Her confidence and self-esteem were shattered bit by bit with each whipping she received as a child.

Decades later, with that young girl carefully put away where I didn't have to think about her, I continued attracting relationships into my life that perpetuated abuse, both emotional and sexual. Because of my intense desire for approval, I drew relationships into my life where I was desperate to please for the love and validation it brought me.

There were many times growing up and even as an adult, when I was told, "there aren't any beauties in our family. We're just average looking people". Constantly being told this kept my self-esteem very low and I carried a very low opinion of myself, which left me struggling in the socially competitive, and occasionally mean atmosphere of traditional schooling, where I endured bullying on a regular basis. When I finished elementary school and started my secondary education, I was overwhelmed with the enormity of the school, the number of people and the high expectations. I often stayed home from school with many imagined illnesses. My parent's eventually gave me permission to leave and I was enrolled in a private girls' school, where I excelled in business studies. They told me it was wise to study and acquire secretarial skills that I could fall back on if I didn't find a husband.

Graduating with honours after two years, I was hired in a receptionist/secretary capacity for a brokerage firm in downtown Toronto. Just after turning seventeen years old, I found myself in my very first relationship with one of the men that I worked for. In his mid-forties, he was over twice my age with children older than me, but his constant interest and kindness towards me, overwhelmed me, as I continued to crave that love and attention. He spent weeks grooming and conditioning me for what was to come. After weeks of lovely, leisurely lunches, small, innocent kisses, a little back rub here and there, he made his move. I found myself in the back of his car, naked and once again, weeping silently following an assault by someone I trusted, respected and looked up to. I wept for my loss of innocence and I wept from overwhelming guilt. A tiny part of me enjoyed parts of it, but the larger part of me was horrified at what had just happened. I was left feeling ashamed – how had I allowed myself to be put into this position?

It wasn't until many years later that I was able to view this through a different lens, and I could see this was sexual abuse by a man who had groomed a child to satisfy his sick sexual appetite. In fact, through the eyes of the law, this would be a criminal offense with a minor. His way of breaking off this very wrong relationship was to let me go from my job very shortly after. Raised in a highly religious environment, I was taught that sex was only for marriage; I was raised to believe I should never allow a man to touch me unless he was my husband. Shame intensified when I considered what my parents would think of me if they found out.

As I continued to search for love and validation to fill the emptiness within me, I met my first husband a few months later at a party I was attending with a friend. We dated just three months before we married. I was seventeen-and-a-half years old. I went into this relationship believing that women should be subservient to their husbands, so I ended up in a very controlling marriage with a man who ruled by the principle, "it's my way or the highway." He would regularly tell me, "If you don't like it, the door swings out". For most of my marriage I fulfilled the role of subservient wife, allowing my husband to dominate me in every aspect of our lives.

My health started spiralling downward, first with chronic bladder problems, then difficulties in carrying pregnancies to term, losing my first son, then miscarriage after miscarriage until I finally was able to carry two of my six pregnancies to term delivering my first full-term baby, a son followed by a daughter three years later.

Nine days after my first child was born, my husband and I were involved in a head on collision with a drunk driver. To this day I thank God that my baby boy was home safe with my mother and not in our car. The car was totalled and I sustained two compound fractures in my neck, a fractured skull and a whiplash along with a concussion which served to compound my already multiplying physical issues.

Illness continued to plague me and at 26 years of age, I underwent a partial hysterectomy for a prolapsed uterus. Three weeks following this major surgery, my husband, playing on my guilt along with my inability to say no, pressured me into sexual intercourse before my six-week healing and recovery period was over. Very shortly after this episode, I began experiencing severe abdominal pain and was rushed to the hospital with cuff cellulitis (a pelvic infection) severe enough that my life was threatened. Lying in emergency in severe pain from the infection, I was immediately put on two different intravenous antibiotics and narcotic painkillers. Within hours, through a morphine-induced haze, I began to feel something was wrong, when I started experiencing swelling of my joints, difficulty breathing and an all-over body rash that as it developed looked like a severe sunburn. This severe allergic reaction to the antibiotics prolonged my recovery by weeks, as changing my medication was necessary along with a course of steroids to manage my allergic reaction, followed by a full eight months of weaning off the corticosteroids.

During the later half of our marriage, as computers and stand-alone word processors started to infiltrate the business world, I decided to go back to college and study computer sciences. After my studies, I applied for and obtained a job in the IT world as a Computer Software Support Specialist. A whole new world opened itself up to me as I discovered a confidence in myself which I had never experienced before. I found my voice which did not bode well in my marriage and it eventually eroded the control my husband had over me and subsequently we ended up divorcing. I was in my early thirties when our marriage of nearly 14 years was over. I left my two children with my husband in our family home so their lives would not be completely turned upside down while I learned how to cope and be alone.

Completely devastated by this decision to separate, I will never forget the day I told my mom and dad. My dad stood up from the table and said, "You know what they will think about a woman who leaves her husband and children" and with that, he left the room. This hurt me deeply and one month after, having not seen my mother or father during that time, my father called me to apologize. That phone call was the call that began the eventual mending of our relationship, which had been nearly destroyed by my ex-husband's need to control me, my relationships, and who I spent time with. I had always been very easily influenced by others, and my husband's constant criticism of my mother and father, how they parented along with everything else he perceived as wrong with them, eventually eroded my relationship, pushing me further away from them.

The period following the breakdown of my marriage continues to be a hazy memory to me. I suffered through terrible loneliness, working many long hours and the loss of my family unit. There were times when the depression and loneliness were so overwhelming, I contemplated taking my life. I couldn't bear the thought of spending the rest of my life in this way.

Six months into my separation, I missed my children terribly, so at Christmas, I spoke with them about moving in with me. I was settled into my apartment; I was settled into my job and I wanted to have my babies with me. My daughter jumped at this opportunity; however, my son wanted to stay with his dad and his friends. So right or wrong, this is what we did. My daughter moved in with me and my son stayed with his dad. The family was further destroyed and two new families were created, which drove a wedge into the relationship between my children, but it also drove a wedge between my son and me. My daughter and her dad eventually lost their relationship as well. These relationships have never been repaired and remain broken to this day. I have accepted that this is the way it is supposed to be, but I thank God every moment for the loving and close relationship I have maintained with my daughter, son-in-law and my grandchildren.

As my daughter and I settled into our life together, I was supported by a few good friends that I worked with. In particular, I developed a close friendship with a wonderful man I had worked with for a few years, and very quickly our friendship grew into love, and we married two years following my divorce.

During the early years of our marriage, I continued climbing the corporate ladder in my profession and within a few years I was hired into a position on a team that was installing one of the first fibre optic networks in Canada. A wonderful opportunity and my dream job, or so I thought. I was the only woman in this Datacom department of six men, and the director of the department was misogynistic, controlling, angry and generally a very mean man. Whenever a project didn't run smoothly, the witch hunt began, and I usually ended up on the chopping block. He seemed to derive great pleasure from regularly bullying, emotionally abusing and keeping me down. I was very intimidated by this man and spent the entire 18 months I worked for him in a high state of nervousness, always anticipating with dread that moment when he would walk into my office.

While working at this firm, I experienced the sudden loss of my beloved grandfather. I asked for and was given two weeks off, but upon returning to work, I was let go. The stress of the time at this job and the loss of my grandfather coupled with the emotionally difficult breakup of my first marriage took a massive toll on my health and within a very short time, my life exploded into pain, chronic depression and disability.

My body continued on its path of several auto-immune diseases that ravaged my health - fibromyalgia, osteoarthritis, rheumatoid arthritis, atypical trigeminal neuralgia, gastric reflux, hiatus hernia, asthma, eczema, pre-diabetes, severe iron deficiency, high cholesterol, chronic depression, lichen sclerosis, and sleep disorders.

I was using over one dozen medications daily to control my chronic pain and depression which interfered with my ability to experience joy in life.

After suffering for years, I started seeing a specialist at a pain clinic where I regularly received trigger point injections with a local anaesthetic to numb my pain. Each session was excruciating, but I did gain a modicum of relief. After a few years of doing this and going to the pain clinic almost daily for pain injections to enable me to get through the hours each day at my stressful job, I asked my doctor to allow me to inject my pain killers myself. I was trained on intramuscular injections by a public health nurse and began self-injecting narcotic pain medication to manage my pain.

In my mid 40's, I was no longer able to hold down a full-time job and I went on disability. It was during this time that I began to realize, life held no joyful future for me and I could not continue on the path I was currently on. So I slowly started investigating, researching and reading everything I could lay my hands on regarding my emotional and physical well-being. And, although I read voraciously and absorbed what I read, something was preventing me from putting it into practice. Deep at the root of my health problems was the little issue of payoff. What was I gaining from remaining ill? Whenever I spoke of my disease and suffering, I naturally received sympathy which served to strengthen my need to cling to my victim mentality.

With my weight now in the obese category, carrying over 230 pounds on my body, I continued to cover up my beautiful authentic self, dimming my light and covering myself in layer after protective layer. By this point, I was even struggling to be mobile without the use of occasional aids.

There was, however, a war raging within me. From the outside, although overweight, I looked relatively healthy. I was embarrassed to appear disabled, yet I thrived on the sympathy and attention it brought me.

At around 46 or 47 years old, I started experiencing terrible digestive problems and it was discovered that the many years of using narcotic pain relievers had severely damaged my digestive system, and now, added to my many health issues was IBS, leaky gut, and severe sensitivities to many, many foods. It became nearly impossible for me to leave my home due to the constant and urgent digestive distress I suffered with. I never knew when it would hit and I needed to stay close to home and my washroom.

Many years later at 50 years old, I was tired and frustrated from conventional medicine telling me the best I could hope for was management of these diseases for the rest of my life. I didn't want to continue existing in a drug-induced fog, taking prescription after prescription that did nothing but numb the pain. Surely there must be a better way to handle my health. So I began investigating alternative medicine and found a naturopathic doctor, in whose office I sat hearing the words, "if you don't make some very drastic changes, you will be a very sick woman by the time you are 60." These words turned my world upside down.

Frightened for what lay ahead of me with my health spiralling downward, I left the doctor's office that day and I found myself in a bookstore perusing the food and lifestyle books. One particular book stood out by author Tosca Reno, entitled "The Eat Clean Diet." Taking this book home, I dove in, devouring every word, and slowly I began incorporating her principles and recipes for clean eating into my life. I gave up dairy, I cut out all white flour, white sugar, white pasta, and white rice. I learned to juice and make green smoothies. My diet consisted of approximately 75-80% fruit and vegetables and over the next eighteen months I slowly shed fifty pounds. I continued eating this way and began incorporating a little movement into my days with Nordic pole walking.

Then, very slowly, I started to wean my body off two antidepressants, disease suppressants for RA, acid blockers for GERD, IBS and a hernia, anti-inflammatories for degenerative arthritis, muscle relaxants for fibromyalgia, steroids and rescue inhalers for asthma, anticonvulsants for trigeminal neuralgia, Parkinson's medication for severe restless leg and regular narcotic injections for pain management. Feeling, clean and clear, I thought: "life is good!"

But as I would soon discover, the Universe was not quite done with me. I still required more softening to prepare me for the growth I was about to experience.

Thus began a new and unknown journey into heart-crushing loss over the next few years. Beginning with the devastating news that my eldest sister was diagnosed with AML (acute myelogenous leukemia) and although she heroically battled for eighteen months, she ultimately lost her battle at the young age of 64. Her death was followed two years later by the passing of my father, who died after suffering for weeks with spasms in his esophagus which prevented him from keeping any food or nourishment in his body. Three short years later (almost to the day) my mother sustained a devastating fall in her studio apartment. She survived her fall; but eventually passed away ten days later due to multiple complications.

Then six weeks to the day after losing my mother, my husband and I lost our beloved fourteen-year-old pup to abdominal cancer.

A week prior to our dog's passing, my husband suggested I go away on a weekend that had been planned for all my brothers and sisters to spend together, taking a day cruise, touring wineries and just enjoying each other's company. Everyone was still very raw from these family deaths, and the weekend turned into a very unpleasant experience where anger was expressed, I felt bullied and endured many nasty comments over why I was so upset about my upcoming loss of my wee girl. "After all it's just a dog!" I heard again and again through the weekend. All this unpleasantness re-awoke long-suppressed memories that began raining down on me like a heavy rainstorm.

Following the death of our sweet girl, I started to fall into a deeper, darker depression. It became so bleak; I could not see any way out. During this time, I was not able to see that these deaths were necessary for my rebirth. Similar to the lotus that grows up through the mud to open its glorious flower, I too had to suffer through my darkness so I could awaken to my beautiful, authentic light. During my depression, I was brought to my knees and for months I found great comfort in my suffering that had me wrapped tightly in a thick blanket. Not wanting to leave this place, I stayed deep in my depression, suffering through the suppressed memories. I was also managing my mother's final wishes and estate, had many dealings with the government for final taxes, death notices, closing of bank accounts, credit cards. All the while, simultaneously dealing with a sibling who constantly pressured me to handle my mother's estate their way. I was barely staying afloat as I worked my way through my grief and many attempts at releasing the suppressed memories that continued to plague my mind.

By allowing trauma and loss to become the focus in my life, by swallowing my emotions – guilt and shame – allowing them to overwhelm me, by holding firmly onto my victim mentality, my body was simply unable to handle any more. All the disease I had suffered had been my messenger telling me that I needed to explore profound change. However, for years, I refused to see my suffering as my messenger. Instead I wallowed in my discomfort and pain, wondering what life had in store for me and my future with all this pain and depression.

As I journeyed alongside my broken self, I slowly awakened to the realization that my physical body could not withstand any more and that I must do some deep diving to release, forgive, accept and surrender.

While I was deep in my grief over these losses, I was totally oblivious to the fact that the Divine was using these circumstances, situations and losses to soften me for the incredible spiritual awakening and healing that would explode into my life just a few months after losing my mom.

One evening while attending a winter solstice celebration, I was introduced to a woman. We spoke at length, and I allowed myself to feel all the emotions around the death of my mother. Feeling safe with her, I let the tears fall. She gently placed her hand on my shoulder and I felt a shock run through my body. It felt like such a foreign sensation that I asked her what it was. She explained to me that she was a Reiki Master. From that moment on, the trajectory of my life changed. It was no longer in my hands, but in the hands of the Divine and I felt deep within me the knowledge that I had come home!

A year of intensive Reiki healing, shared Reiki circles and study put me on the fast-track to healing my emotional wounds, learning to forgive myself and others, I was learning to love myself.

And in learning the value of loving myself, I found the love that I felt for others magnified exponentially. My heart opened, and I knew what it meant to truly, authentically and unconditionally love others. New and beautiful souls were attracted to me as I quickly learned that LOVE was what I was now projecting. I found myself giving gratitude for every single breath . . . every single moment . . . every single thing.

In just over four years, I was honoured, through hard work and copious amounts of study to achieve and receive the level of Reiki Master/Teacher/Practitioner firmly cementing my path to share this beautiful gift with others. Today I offer deep gratitude for each and every illness, every loss, every disease, grief and suffering because it brought me to this point. Had I not gone through those times of darkness,

I would not have been able to recognize the beautiful light I was now bathed in.

Through the many years of my journey, I worked diligently to fall in love with me, with all my 'flawsomeness', with all the different parts of me - my shadow side, my light side, my too wide hips, my luscious curves, my warrior, my victim, my manipulator, my puritan, my mother energy, my daughter energy, but most importantly my woman energy.

Accepting and learning to love myself coupled with an attitude of gratitude became my all-consuming journey towards my healing.

Learning to love myself – well it was and still is painful, exquisite, devastating and rewarding with many emotional twists, turns, shifts and aha moments. As I dug deep, I released anger, resentment, judgement; I fully surrendered to the Divine, and I embraced gratitude. I experienced many more losses in those early years but as those doors closed, I was able to see and absorb the lessons provided for my emotional and spiritual growth. And there were so many more doors that were waiting to open!

After spending many years locked in anger, resentment and judgement of not only myself but others, I had attracted the same type of individuals back into my life. Years of soul-searching and many tearful episodes face to face with myself in front of my mirror, brought me to a place of acceptance, getting comfortable in my own skin and owning my lusciousness. Now, I can truly say, "I live my life with complete joy". And this all started with "finding love for myself". I live a life of abundance because I found deep and unconditional LOVE for myself.

In 2015, I challenged myself to give gratitude in a public forum every day for the entire year. Doing this was profoundly life-changing for me as I saw myself slowly moving into an attitude of gratitude with the passing of each and every day. My gratitude journey has forever altered my life. I went on to give gratitude in this public forum for a full three years, that's 1095 days!! Gratitude has been and continues to be the cornerstone upon which I build my life. I remain steadfast with my gratitude posts regularly, not always every day this year, but I express my gratitude in small posts on Facebook as the spirit moves me. Now, when I face pain, loss or difficult situations, it is not with a "why me" attitude, but through the eyes of gratitude; always searching for the lessons that are being provided for my ultimate growth.

I am no longer defined by my story, but with a deep understanding and profound gratitude for the people, situations, circumstances, events, losses, and illness that were provided; to show me what I needed to learn in order to grow to where I am today.

Today as a Master Healer/Teacher/Practitioner, I am honoured to offer myself as a healer and teacher. I am blessed to embrace my students and lovingly mentor them; passing this beautiful gift of Reiki on to them as they also journey through this gift of healing.

I am passionate about inspiring and empowering other women to embrace their own healing; and last year I created a signature event, "An Exceptional Woman." This event is to inspire, motivate, and empower women to build on their past pain as the pedestal to the pinnacle of their purpose, and to celebrate their exceptional self.

Profound change is possible and it is within your grasp. I am living proof that someone who only eight short years ago wrote in her journal, "I need to learn to love myself and not depend upon others for my own happiness".

Marianne Williamson says, "Our deepest fear is not that we are inadequate. Our deepest fear is that we are powerful beyond measure. It is our light, not our darkness that most frightens us. We ask ourselves, who am I to be brilliant, gorgeous, talented and fabulous? My question is, "who are we not to be brilliant, gorgeous, talented and fabulous?"

Remember that little girl who sat weeping silently on her bed – feeling unworthy, unloved, not good enough, hating herself and living her life wrapped in anger and resentment? Well she is still there, but I have embraced her, I have loved her and I have forgiven her. I have released the judgement of her and in coming home, she has found her magnificent light.

COMING HOME

*The pain of the past, simmering just beneath the face she
exposed to the world
Always there, churning and bubbling,
Destroying her self-esteem, her morals, her thoughts, her
abilities.
Deeper and deeper they went until she couldn't recognize
them any longer.*

*What happened to this woman, what hurts, what pain, what
grief that left her wanting health, happiness and freedom
from the pain.
How deep must she dig to release this pain?
Can she find what she seeks?*

*She experienced abuse, she experienced death, the sting of
cruelty from a friend,
the bite of hate within her family.
All working together to create that fertile ground for every
negative emotion,
Anger, resentment, self-loathing, judgement, bitterness, envy.
This girl was good for no one
But then one day her whole life changed
She was brought to the edge but could she take the next step
What was waiting beyond?
Forgiveness, acceptance, self-love, humility, all within her
reach, yet was she ready to release the past?*

*The cloak of grief and depression were wrapped tightly
around her.
They had her locked within their grips.
They comforted her, they eased her pain, protected her from
the world.
But was she ready to drop these crutches – NO!
Deep within she knew she must let them drop from her body
as leaves must drop from the trees in autumn.*

*Shifting, awakening, changing at her core, releasing ego,
piety, anger, resentment. The list was painfully long.
The pain was moving upwards and outwards - breaking the
surface,
Wearing her down, reliving and reminding her of the
trauma.
How low her vibrations were, but now they were rising
She felt a difference in her soul.
She loved, she laughed, she was embracing the wholeness of
life.*

*Reiki became part of her journey introduced to her one
winter solstice night.
She felt the pulsing energy and knew she was home.
Her searching was done and a new spiritual life opened to
her.
The fear of death was gone - replaced with peacefulness.
The horrors of a cruel God - replaced with a Divine source
of unconditional love.
She pondered her lives, previously and yet to come.*

How many lives had she lived, how many more would she live?
What gifts had she given, what gifts had she to offer the world?

A new life was hers and was within her reach.
The hurts were all gone, replaced with unconditional all-inclusive love.
How did she exist so long unaware, living but not quite alive?
Reiki had brought her such joy, and she would forever be grateful for that winter solstice night, when she felt the energy in that hand on her shoulder.
Waking her up, changing her core, filling her up.
She truly had come home .... Barb Takeda

The Courage to Change

THE UNSPOKEN SIDE OF MOTHERHOOD

The Courage to Change

Joya Williams-Murray

Joya Williams-Murray is married with two beautiful daughters. She started writing as a teenager and has always had a love of words. But it wasn't until later in life that she started to actually think of herself as a writer. She found the courage to share her writing with others; exposing a very private part of herself and opening herself up to criticism. Joya's blog "Super Mom Doesn't Live Here' is her ode to motherhood and the messy, imperfect life she leads as a mom. In addition to blogging, she also writes short story fiction and has been published in online publications like shortfictionbreak.com.

She has also edited and co-edited several independent writing projects. Her next goal is to finish her first novel, and be an example to her children of what can be accomplished when you stop being afraid to pursue the things you are passionate about.

Raising A Mother
by Joya Williams-Murray

I sat on the couch in my living room, watching TV. Sudden flutters of movement in my belly caused me to rest a hand on what seemed to be my ever-growing body. My baby was moving. I loved that feeling more than I can even describe. My 'peanut' was in there. That was the nickname we had given the baby. We had no idea if it was a boy or a girl, but of course, everyone had their opinion. I carried like a boy; my hair was growing so it must have been a boy, but then someone else dreamt that I was carrying a girl and so it went. "Oh, you're going to have a big baby!" other people told me. I was scared.

This was my first pregnancy, and I had heard the horror stories about 36-hour labours, C-sections, tearing and all the other gory details. It's funny how people tend to volunteer this unsolicited information, utterly oblivious to the panic they instil in you. But as I sat on my couch that day, I remember thinking, "Can I really do this?" A sudden feeling of fear came over me as I realized that I would be responsible for another human being's life. That they would depend on me to care for them, protect them and guide them in life. Ironic though, because I still hadn't figured out my own life. How was I going to give advice to someone else?

I found out early on in the pregnancy that I had a small tear in my placenta. Of course, that worried me too. At one of my appointments, I asked my family doctor at what point could I stop worrying about miscarriages? "A miscarriage can happen at any time," he said to me gently. I didn't realize how naïve I really was. So on top of worrying whether I could be a good mother, I also worried about how I would protect the life inside of me. I was so nervous I didn't say anything for the first few weeks of my pregnancy, not even to my closest friend; because if something terrible happened, then there would be more people affected...disappointed. It seemed to make sense at the time. Little did I realize that the worry would never really go away. My mother always says that no matter how old your kids are, you still worry about them. She also said, "one day when you have kids, you'll understand."

Peanut

When I went into labour, it went a lot faster than I expected. My daughter came into the world in a hurry, and she hasn't slowed down. She's almost a teenager and gives her younger sister a hard time every chance she gets. I find myself watching her and remembering the days when I would sit in a softly-lit nursery in the glider, with her in my arms and just cry. Her father was asleep in the other room while silent tears ran down my face. I couldn't do this. I couldn't care for this tiny baby. I was tired. I was scared, and I had no idea what I was doing. Breastfeeding was a lot harder than anyone cared to mention. And I was so damn *tired*.

That first week when she came home from the hospital, I was so busy trying to figure out what to do. I'm not sure I took a moment just to enjoy her. My mother came over every day, and although I was grateful for her being there, I also felt as if I was lacking in some way because she was able to calm the baby in ways that I had yet to learn.

My boyfriend (now husband) took time off work to be there for me, but I'm not sure I relied on him the way I should have because it was *my* job to be her mother. *I* had to do this. But almost every night in that glider in the early hours of the morning, I would sit there and cry. I'm not sure how long this went on for, but then one of those lonely nights as I fed her and listened to the soft snores coming from the other room, I brought her to my chest to rub her back, and I felt the familiar wetness on my cheeks. I stopped gliding and just sat reclining with her in the stillness with my eyes closed. Suddenly, she began to wriggle her way up my chest; it seemed like only a few inches at a time, but she kept moving. Instinctively, I adjusted the way I was holding her and moved her up so that her head was resting on my shoulder. She moved her head back ever so slightly and inhaled. I can't describe the feeling, and some may not understand it. But my daughter inhaled, sighed, then fell asleep; and at that moment I knew love like I had never known before. I was so grateful for her that the tears falling down my face were happy ones, instead of the ones that belonged to someone so unsure of herself. I was her mother, and I would do anything and everything to protect her.

It still wasn't easy, and maybe I was too proud to ask for the help that I needed. My mother helped me even when I didn't think I needed it, for which I am truly grateful because raising a tiny human being is probably the most rewarding but emotionally exhausting thing I'll ever do.

My boyfriend and I settled into a routine or at least tried to. There were moments where we were very close but also times that felt strained. I think he just assumed that I had it all figured out and that if I didn't say anything, then I didn't need anything. Like waiting for me to get up in the middle of the night when she woke up crying. When I complained, he would say, "Well, why didn't you wake me?" But when I did, he would say, "Ok" then roll over and go back to sleep. Or pretend to, because I still don't believe he slept through all of it. No way. There were times when I would leave the baby with him so that I could run some errands or just have some time to myself. He would get annoyed with all the instructions I left, but then an hour later I would get a phone call to ask me when I was coming home; his voice filled with exasperation or some days panic. Then on the days when he would call to say that he was stopping for a beer with the guys, I don't think it ever occurred to him that I might have been feeling as overwhelmed after a full day with the baby as he did after an hour or two.

Because I had done a lot of reading throughout my pregnancy, at some point, I realized that I was suffering from postpartum depression.

"I can't stop crying," I told my doctor, "I think I'm depressed." He'd been my doctor since I was sixteen years old and I could always trust him to be frank.

"Postpartum depression can last up to two years," he said gently. "As long as you don't feel like you would want to hurt yourself or the baby, it is normal." I didn't know how this feeling could be considered normal, but then again, I guessed I was pretty lucky that it wasn't more severe. That didn't make it any easier. So I continued to cry, thinking that perhaps it was cleansing and I told myself that crying was allowing me to release all of these feelings of loneliness and failure. But also hurt and anger. Those feelings were directed towards my partner because I felt as if he had absolutely no clue how hard all of this was for me, nor did he care. I thought that he had found me lacking, and I had already found that in myself. I felt hurt that he expected me to be 'normal' when nothing felt that way. I was exhausted!

I felt guilty at every turn because I didn't know what I was doing. I felt useless when it seemed like my mother and everyone else I knew seemed to know what to do. Why didn't anyone tell me having a baby would be this hard? We struggled. All of a sudden, we weren't who we used to be. It took a lot of work and talking to each other to get back to a place where we were both comfortable. It was then that I realized that he thought I was doing fine and never recognized that I felt like I was drowning. But I also never knew that he suddenly felt left out of the equation and no longer an essential focus in my life. It was an important discovery for both of us. However, this is something that we wouldn't talk about *for a while.*

But through all of this, I knew I wanted another baby. I was open about my postpartum depression. Although I had never been diagnosed, it wasn't hard to figure out that I wasn't myself. I spoke about it the same way someone discusses the weather. And maybe that was the problem. I wasn't necessarily crying out for help. "How are you?" or "How are you handling everything?" people would ask me. Depending on the day, my answer would be "Fine, I'm getting used to it," or "It's exhausting. I'm tired all the time." As simple and straightforward as "It's raining outside." I may not have looked like someone who was going through it. So people treated me as they usually would. I tried my best to be *normal*.

At some point, I stopped crying and became more confident about what my daughter needed from me. I wasn't perfect by any means, but I was doing the best that I could, and my love for her knew no bounds.

Baby Girl

Finding out I was pregnant again was a moment of joy but also a conduit to more emotional stress. I worried about taking care of a toddler and being pregnant, and wondered how on earth I could share the love that I had for my daughter with another child. I didn't want to be one of those parents that had favourites. I didn't want to be the cause of a child growing up with low self-esteem. How would I manage all of this? What made me think I could do this? It's a question I asked myself over and over. My insecurities led me to doubt myself and my partner once again. We argued about everything. *Everything*.

Our daughter came two weeks early, and we found out that she had jaundice. She was so tiny, only 5lbs 12oz at birth. I was told that I would have to bring her back to the postnatal clinic once a week to do bloodwork and check her body weight. At my first appointment with the postnatal nurse, I was told once again how vital breastfeeding would be for her, especially because of the jaundice. The nurse was very stern, which was new for me because up until that point, all the nurses that had helped me during both labours were really friendly. She asked me about my breastfeeding experience the first time, and I told her about the difficulties that I had. She immediately told me what I had done wrong the last time and what I should be doing this time around.

The only problem was that baby #2 was a very sleepy baby and would fall asleep during feedings. She advised me to use a cold cloth on the bottom of her feet to wake her up. We also noticed that she wasn't always latching on and so she gave me a contraption with a small tube attached that I was supposed to put in the baby's mouth once I started to breastfeed. Apparently, this would allow her to get milk from the tube which she would then associate with latching on and then it should be fine from there on out. However, balancing a baby and getting the tube in her mouth at the same time was not an easy task. Almost impossible, I might add, even with help. As a result, she wasn't eating as much as she should have, and at my next appointment, the nurse was very angry with me. Which did nothing to help the anxiety I was already feeling. She told me very firmly that if I couldn't get her to feed and start gaining weight, that she would have to admit her to the hospital and she would stay there for up to 6 weeks. Maybe she thought I wasn't trying or that I was lazy or something, but the threat hit home as I'm sure she hoped it would.

"No wonder you had trouble the first time." She said, seemingly annoyed. I started to cry. She had no idea how much she hurt me with those words.

"Oh no, don't cry," she said. "It will get easier."

That was the only time she was actually a bit nice to me. I cried all the way home. I couldn't fail my child. I had to get it right this time. I called my mother to tell her what the nurse said.

"Take that baby outside for some sun and if you need to give her a bottle then just give it to her, she said.

"But the nurse told me to keep her out of the sun and to only breastfeed her or she won't latch properly," I said still crying.

"Well, back home, we would have sat outside to give her some sun, and we would have given her some sugar and water to help her put on some weight." She told me over the phone. "Don't let that nurse scare you."

So the next morning, I wrapped my baby girl in a blanket (in the middle of July), and I sat on the bench in front of our townhouse. There was enough shade to make sure she wasn't directly in the sun, but still get some benefit from it. I left her feet out to feel the warm breeze, and she kicked her little legs immediately. I did that for the next week. I still worked at trying to breastfeed, but I also pumped and fed her from the bottle to make sure she was getting enough.

By the time the next postnatal appointment came around, my daughter was eating well from the breast and the bottle, but I was still nervous.

"I'm glad to see you've been following my advice." The nurse said after weighing her and doing the necessary bloodwork to monitor her jaundice. She had put on weight, and the jaundice was gone. I had listened to my mother and to my own instincts.

I gave her a hard stare and said, "Yup." That was the last time I saw that nurse, but that experience stayed with me.

The jaundice was gone, but my postpartum came back nearly twice as bad as the first time. Even so, it was time to get back into a routine. Her big sister needed my attention, and I needed her big sister to remind me that I knew what I was doing. I had done this once before, I could do it again. I had my mother to help me as she had been up to that point, and my partner was there to pick up the slack when I needed him to. But even with all of the help around me, there was a constant sadness that I couldn't shake; I cried all the time.

I was determined this time around to breastfeed longer than 3 months. To get more sleep and to do all the things I had struggled with the first time. It all seemed to be working out until I developed a yeast infection. Seriously? Up there? So here I was almost at the three-month mark, and I had adjusted a lot better to breastfeeding, I was starting to feel like a bit of a pro. Don't get me wrong, it still hurt sometimes, and Baby Girl had a habit of clamping down just to let me know she was finished. I can still feel the sensation of one leg kicking right out as a reflex every time she did it. Ugh.

So when I started to feel this burning sensation on my breasts, I did what I was supposed to do. I went to the doctor, and then I called the free breastfeeding clinic to get advice. They told me just to keep going. That it would get better but just keep going.

I don't remember if the doctor gave me anything to get rid of the yeast. But what I do remember is one day getting home from dropping my older daughter off at daycare. My mother was watching the little one, and I could hear her screaming at the top of her little lungs before I put the key in the lock.

"She's hungry," my mother said, "but she wants you, not the bottle." I moved quickly. Kicking my shoes off and running into the kitchen to wash my hands. I hurriedly lifted my top to pull the latch on my breastfeeding bra and felt immediate pain. Looking down on the bra and the disposable pad inside it, I saw patches of my skin where there should have only been dried milk. My right breast was raw and bleeding, but my daughter was still crying. So I clipped my bra back in place and gently pulled down the left side; even in pain I fed her and then fed her from the bottle she had refused earlier to top her up.

Calm now, she drank what she didn't want before. While I sat watching and wondering how mothering could be so hard sometimes. I was in pain and in love with my daughter at the same time. But the knowledge that this yeast infection existed made me feel like a failure. I don't remember anyone telling me how hard breastfeeding would be. At least not until after I had struggled with it and started talking to other mothers. I had a few friends that said, "Oh no, I had no issues with it." But I had more friends that said "Hell ya, it was hard and it hurt like hell at the beginning!" or "Girl...I tried, but I couldn't do it." So why had I never heard this until now?

Talking to people, my mom, other mothers, became my most significant help. It made me feel normal and helped me to forgive myself for things I didn't know or couldn't control. It made me laugh when my friends would share their own anecdotes about breastfeeding or other things that their bodies went through. I needed that so much. I never realized how much until I started asking questions and learned that most moms out there were just as scared and unsure as I was.

Where Am I?

After the second baby, I felt heavy and unattractive. All of my other friends seemed to lose their baby weight without issue. But once I stopped breastfeeding, my weight seemed to disperse itself in peculiar ways, and I felt like a blob. Every time I looked in the mirror, I wanted to cry. What happened to me? Where was I? I definitely wasn't in the reflection I stared at every day. I was stuck in this new role with no access to my former self. I didn't like it, but I didn't know how to change it. Besides, I was barely coping with motherhood, what was the point of trying to do anything else? However, the unhappiness I felt started to seep into my relationships, my expressions and the way I carried myself. My clothes didn't fit, and my hair was breaking after pregnancy. I felt ugly, and I remember telling myself that I *was* ugly. Even as I told my 3-year-old every day how beautiful she was. I wanted her to have the self-esteem her mother didn't have.

Looking back now, I realize that depression (postpartum or otherwise) is a very deceptive condition and affects everyone differently. I didn't lock myself in a dark room for days or have thoughts of hurting myself or my children. I functioned quite well actually. I got up every day and took care of my kids. I took my oldest to daycare, and I went to the Mommy and Me Zumba and yoga classes. I took the baby to the mall so I could shop, I went for walks and out for coffee with my mother or my friends. To the outside world, I was doing just fine. But when I stepped into the shower at night, all of my pain and depression was let loose under the spray. Every last ounce of it. I told myself that I was a bad mother, a failure, ugly, fat, and whatever else I was feeling that day. I would put my face in the water and wash away my tears and soothe my burning eyelids. Then I'd get out and go to bed.

I knew something needed to change, but I didn't know what and it made me angry when my boyfriend would say things like "If you don't like how you look, maybe you should join a gym." He would even bring home the flyers from various gyms in the area. He was trying to encourage me to stop complaining and start doing something, and it pissed me right off. I mean, who the hell did he think he was? Did he even know about my life? Was he paying attention to the crap I was dealing with? Because, of course, I expected him to just get it. But he didn't, and it made me mad. I told him that I was feeling depressed, but in our culture, people didn't talk about depression. You were either tired or sick, or maybe you just needed some tea. But talking about depression was foolishness, and so his response was to hug me and tell me that I was "all right."

I wasn't, but it was an improvement for him because, after my first pregnancy, all we did was fight.

"Sometimes, I feel like I'm failing as a mother," I said to him more than once.

"No. You're not. Your kids are healthy and loud and happy. You are fine." He would say as I cried on his shoulder. Those days he helped me much more than taking over diaper duty, but I didn't tell him that. He would have loved to get out of changing those diapers!

One day I finally mentioned to a friend that I felt out of shape, and I didn't know how to lose the baby weight. She invited me to check out the boot camp class that she was taking. I was hesitant at first, mainly because I felt insecure about how I looked, and the last thing I needed was to be in a room full of fit, hot-bodied women in their booty shorts and sports bras while I waddled around in my boyfriend's old t-shirts and a pair of my baggiest sweatpants. I would look and feel out of place. But she reassured me that it was a very welcoming atmosphere and that the instructor was very helpful.

She was right. The class was great but hard. Most of the time I felt like I was going to pass out, but I stuck with it. Other people noticed my accomplishments long before I did. I was too busy trying to keep up with the classes to realize or even appreciate my success. But I felt great.

I also joined a writing workshop. It had been a long time since I'd taken one or exposed myself to criticism about my writing. But it forced me to write regularly. It took me a little outside of my daily routine once a week. I didn't write about motherhood. I wrote about pain and revenge. It was oddly healing, being able to express myself without having to be positive all the time. I wrote about angry women in one aspect or another and how they coped or overcame whatever they were going through.

Forgiving Myself

A friend once told me that "everything is a phase." We were talking about our kids, and I was regaling a group of moms with stories of rebellion that were happening in my house between myself and my eight-year-old. It was advice that her aunt had given her and had helped her cope with the

120

changes that her daughters went through. It is a saying that I have never forgotten and when I find myself in a battle of wills with one of the girls, it quickly comes to mind. It also makes me realize that, even at the beginning of my journey as a mother, the struggles and self-doubt were all a phase too. Even the postpartum depression to some degree.

The expectations I had put on myself to be the perfect mom had taken a heavy toll on me. But I know I'm not the only one. As women, it is taken for granted that motherhood will come naturally to us. We will know exactly what to do and when. Why would we be tired or depressed? Just take a nap when the baby is sleeping. Easy as 1-2-3. Maybe it is for some women, but for a lot more women, it's harder than people actually realize. Until we start talking about it.

At some point, I started forgiving myself for not being a perfect mom. I don't think I consciously set out to be perfect, but there must have been some small hidden part of me that thought I should be, or else why would I be so hard on myself? Why would I be so consumed with guilt when things weren't perfect? Like having a spotless house even though I was exhausted. Or dinner ready every day like clockwork or losing that baby weight in record time like some of the other moms at the 'baby & me Zumba' classes? Why do some moms seem to have it all together when others are struggling? I wonder now if they really had it all together or if they were crying inside and silently screaming for help. Maybe they had different expectations for themselves, and so they had no reason to feel so insecure about their abilities as a mother.

The good thing about experience is that at some point, your knowledge catches up with your emotions, and you function well at your job without even realizing it. I'm not sure when I stopped measuring myself against unreasonable expectations of what my role as a mother should be, but I found my comfort in motherhood and in marriage. It's not a perfect situation by any means, but when I begin to beat myself up about things that I may not have accomplished, I have a few things that are my go-to salves for the spirit.

Prayer, first of all, is for me a soothing and strengthening of my heart. Family gets me through every day. My kids make me laugh, cry, yell and question my sanity, and they love me and forgive me for the mistakes I inevitably make. My husband drives me crazy and makes me so angry sometimes, but he also supports me and gets annoyed when I forget to be kind to myself. My mother will drop everything to help me when I ask, and when I don't, she finds ways to give unconditional love and support. She thinks she's being subtle, but she doesn't have a subtle bone in her body. I not only love my family but I *like* my family, I like spending time with them and even when I need a little me time, I still can't wait to get back to the chaos.

Friends help me not to take myself so seriously and allow me to erase all of my frustration and insecurity. They commiserate with me, they listen to my problems and give me advice and tell me in different ways to not be so hard on myself. My closest friends know when I am at the edge and need to be pulled back from the brink of harsh self-judgment. So the saying "it takes a village to raise a child" may sound cliché, but in reality, it also applies to 'raising a mother.'

Without the support of those who care for me and love me, I could not be the mother that I am. I could not have come through the other side of being a new mother and dealing with uncertainty, unending exhaustion, postpartum depression and the drastic lifestyle changes that having children brings.

I will never be the perfect mom. Sometimes I forget school events, birthday party invitations, special school lunch requests and other stuff. I get angry, and I worry too much. I still cry at times, but we all have bad days. I remember to tell my kids that I love them, I pray every day that I will be the mother that they need me to be. I say "I'm sorry" when I'm wrong and tell my girls that I make mistakes too. I play dolls and dance to Disney tunes with my little one or the latest hit on the radio. I tell stories and terrible jokes, I sing off key and totally embarrass my soon-to-be teen (on purpose). I hold them when they are sad or scared, I fall asleep in the middle of the night with them in my arms or by my side when they need comfort and no matter how crazy things get, I always try to remember to stop and listen when something just doesn't seem right.

I won't always be at my best, but I'm doing the best that I can. There are no manuals that can teach what it means to be a mother. No course to show how to calm or comfort, to guide or to love a child. Those days in the glider wondering if I could do this seem so far away now.

I am doing this. It's called motherhood.

The Courage to Change

Lynn Milne

Lynn Milne is the Co-Founder of The Harmonious Gypsys, a Reiki II practitioner, VoxxLife Associate, and Soul Adventure Game Facilitator.

After struggling for years with fibromyalgia and finally having no choice but to leave a job in the corporate world she absolutely loved, Lynn Milne Renzetti found herself stranded without any medical answers and without an identity. How do you define your worth when it has been defined for you in all the years you worked for someone else?

The road to reinventing Lynn Milne Renzetti has been wrought with depression, confusion and many dead ends - especially in trying to figure out how she may be able to contribute to her family's financial situation and leave a legacy for her sons that she can be proud of. The last place she ever imagined was working for herself, as herself. If authenticity has a name today, it is upheld by those who truly work to serve others.

In the last few years, Lynn has grown beyond recognizing her former self; joining VoxxLife as an Independent Associate with her own wearable neurotech distribution centre based out of Durham region; helping people in pain change the quality of their lives.

In late 2018 co-founding the company The Harmonious Gypsys, a lifelong dream of another powerful woman in her own right; together they have created a Travelling Caravan to serve those beginning their spiritual journey as well as those well on their own way - offering homemade and handmade basics from their gardens, Oracle and Soul Adventure reading parties as well as up-cycled clothing and treasures picked up along their travels - all to inspire and bring out the Gypsy in you.

And finally, after much self-discovery and personal work with different coaches, Lynn is one of the founding facilitators for the Soul Adventure - Journey to the Real Me game.

Lynn believes that transformation is not possible without growth, growth is not possible without a strong foundation, so when you find a community that provides both, you find yourself again.

The Gifts Within My Darkness
by Lynn Milne

There is absolutely no doubt in my mind that depression is a thief. It took me years, and tears, and more years to come to realize that it can also be a gift. My first real awareness of depression came after the difficult pregnancy and birth of my firstborn son. No matter what I had been through during the pregnancy, I could not wait to meet him, visualizing how incredible our happy family would be. I knew I had been through enough that I could take on whatever a newborn could throw at me. What I didn't count on was my own body somehow reconfiguring the message, turning me into someone even I couldn't recognize.

When my first son was born early and humongous (three weeks early and 10lbs 2oz), he and I both went through a pretty traumatic birth. I knew something was wrong the minute we got home, and the next day we were back in the hospital for a week (me with an infection, but more importantly him with jaundice bad enough that he was in an incubator under triple lights). I loved that little man something fierce, but I also knew that I was off kilter somehow. Everyone, my obstetrician included, chalked it up to him being early, being big, the trauma, the healing, etc., etc. I knew about the baby blues, but I also knew that they shouldn't last for more than a few weeks. I was going crazy, slowly, and no one was listening.

I can remember sitting on the couch with him wearing the same pyjamas I had been in for days, staring at the tv but seeing nothing; not caring about doing anything except feeding, changing and rocking him to sleep over and over and over. It was like I was trapped behind a plastic wall, covered in some kind of glue, and stumbling through a fog. The weight of despair that could not be voiced or understood, almost buried me.

I couldn't sleep, I didn't care if I ate, and bathing didn't even cross my radar. When my husband came home from work, I would hand the baby over and just cry at how easy it seemed to be for my husband to be happy. When we went to his parents, or my parents, anywhere really, I bounced between guilty relief of having other people to look after the baby and the furiously infuriating feeling that people kept taking my baby from me. I knew deep down that neither was the right emotion, but I didn't quite understand what I was feeling or how to express it without getting angry or crying inconsolably.

I was embarrassed to seem so emotionally unbalanced. I lost interest in everything, and since my son was a November baby, there was no motivation to get outside and enjoy the fresh air. Although, I doubt if he had been born in the summer, it would have made any difference.

When I finally made it to my own regular doctor, I sat in a stupor. But the fog began to lift somewhat as she ticked off symptoms one after the other being so deep in the woods, I had not been able to see the forest for the trees. I knew I was lost somehow but had no idea that what I was going through was something that could be diagnosed and treated. With the proper combination of antidepressants and a referral to a psychologist who worked with me, introducing me to Cognitive Behavioral Therapy and other modalities that could be used for most types of depression, I was back to a healthier physical and emotional me within a couple of weeks. But postpartum depression doesn't just go away that easily; mentally, I was in a whole different ball game.

For a long time, the stigma from previous generations where mental health was seen as a weakness, weighed heavily on me. Here I was, a successful career woman making over six figures, and I couldn't keep it together when it seemed to me like sixteen-year-olds had kids with no problem. The judgement I piled on myself was harsh, the comparisons to other moms were brutal and cruel. The guilt was sometimes suffocating. And I chose, unconsciously at the time, and obviously so that I could be grateful for it now, to allow others to compound all of these feelings and beliefs I had piled on myself; I saw only my failure in their success. It was proof to me that I wasn't good enough or worthy enough or mentally capable as a mother. It was easy to tear myself apart and let my wounds fester, the feelings of guilt and shame a true part of me because all I had to compare myself to was the perfection I perceived in other moms.

Postpartum depression (as well as my continual battle with depression as a whole) grows like ivy, tiny tendrils of doubt and shame creeping into tiny cracks and clinging – fortifying the foundation, but destroying it at the same time. It takes whatever it can get its claws into – body, mind and spirit. It plucks away bit by bit to the very core of who you are until you no longer know who you really are. The ordeal that I actually went through with the pregnancy and birth had repercussions that lasted for at least two years afterwards (and intermittently since then). Depression is crafty at disguise; rolling over you like crashing waves during a massive storm or creeping in stealthily like a sunburn after a great day at the beach. It leaves you in pain and bewilderment – you were so sure you did everything to prevent it from happening, but there it was anyway.

At the time, (and usually every time since), I went through what I went through with a smile on my face in public, while I was falling apart on the inside. Having postpartum depression go undiagnosed and misdiagnosed for over three months by a professional whose practice it is to deal with such issues on a daily basis was enough to send my fragile state of being over the deep end. Knowing there was something wrong, but being dismissed by an authority I trusted made me feel like it was all in my head; like I was a failure as a mother before I was even given a chance to try. I know now that I am not the only one who struggles with this, but I also know that in this struggle, each of us feels like we are utterly alone.

It was also unbearably hard to see and be around, so many other moms (my sisters-in law, my friends, even strangers) who seemed to have a handle on everything and didn't look like the life was being sucked out of them. I didn't understand why I was having such a hard time; I loved my boy beyond measure and wanted so desperately to measure up and do right by him. And while I did not blame them necessarily, it was very difficult to be around other moms because seeing them deal with motherhood so easily made me feel even more unworthy. Until I was finally diagnosed, I seriously thought I was going mad, that I was the only one dealing with what I was going through, and that I had no one to turn to.

What our mind can process during depression is 'who wants to be around a friend who is bummed out for no apparent reason?' Most of what we are taught is to surround ourselves with people who lift us up, who give us positive energy. But sometimes energy just isn't enough. And we know that no one wants to be around someone whose energy is so low, it doesn't even register on the scale. So, we spend the energy we do have putting on our best voice, our best face for those that need us, for those that call or that we meet up with. It is not like we want to act like we have it all together (although that can sometimes help us), it is more that we don't want to take away from anyone else's joy or add to their burdens.

We spend a lot of energy so that no one sees us when we are sometimes screaming so loudly: *why doesn't anyone see me?*. How do you say "Hey, I'm having a bad day, can you help me out, even though I don't even know what kind of help I need? Did you not know from how I was acting or not acting?" Which one of our friends or family would we want to burden with all this when they all already have enough on their plate to deal with? And then we add on the guilty burden of thinking which one of our friends or family will say, "well, why didn't you come to me?"

Depression is a struggle because we ourselves do not know how to deal with it. We are in a world we have never been in before, underwater, not wanting to admit we are drowning, not wanting to drag anyone down with us, but desperately needing the help that we have no clue how to ask for. It is a stigma because we think there is something wrong with us, and that we are the only ones having such a hard time dealing.

It was two and a half years later that my second gorgeous monster baby was born. Early, again, and even bigger than his older brother at 12lbs 10oz, he lived up to his namesake, Bringer of Light. Even as a "preemie" who was rushed down to Sick Kids with an enlarged heart (while I went to Scarborough Centenary with spinal meningitis from the epidural), he brought smiles to everyone who saw and took care of him while I was out of commission.

I can remember going into the hospital on the morning of his planned c-section, May 1st, thinking of the jokes I could make up - like "On the day you were born, I was yelling out May Day, May Day!" How little did I know the irony then. You see, I had thought I was fully prepared for my old friend depression to come creeping in to take over in my place. Well, let's back up to the fact that I even entertained the thought of getting pregnant again considering what I had gone through the first time around. When we found out we had another bruiser on the way, I took precautionary steps to make sure I was in the right place in both my head and my physical self so that I would know to jump all over the depression if it even dared to rear its ugly head.

And although I only saw him for a second after he was born and again briefly as he was wheeled off to an ambulance in an incubator, my second son was what lit my way while we lay in separate hospitals for the first week of his life. This time around I had prepared for what might sneak in: the signs, the feelings, the soft whisper of fear, overwhelm, the loud hammering of not good enough - especially after another challenging and traumatic birth for both of us. But depression isn't really a test you can prepare for, and as I have said, she is crafty and waits for the perfect time to start messing with you. Like when you are resting in your hospital bed knowing both you and your child are in safe hands. Until your roommate gets to hold her baby, and you hear the loving parents, behind a curtain of course, because that makes it so much easier to bear, gush about how perfect their newborn is and how they were both going to be released later that day. In creeps the panic attack, the one I think I know how to deal with.

Except my baby wasn't down the hall in neonatal, he was downtown at Sick Kids hospital - so far out of my reach, with only a snapshot, spinal meningitis, pain in my head as if someone were trying to tear it in half with needle nose pliers, and a medically induced haze to keep me company. Oh, and of course my good friend depression is happy to keep me company both day and night, ready to creep into my dreams and wrap her arms around me, rocking me into the comfort zone she created after the birth of my first child.

The day my second son was born, the earth had still not woken from its winter slumber; maybe it was a foreshadowing of what the day would bring to both of us. But how strong you were, my beautiful light, how you charmed the nurses so that they would come to visit you even when their shifts were over. How you stayed calm with tubes and wires and pokes and prods - how proud everyone was to hold you and tell me what a bruiser you were. I know they meant well, but my friend depression did its best, taunting me with how everyone else got to see him, to hold him before I did. Did I really think I was going to get off easy this time around? I can't even count how many times I wept the week we were apart. For not being there again to be able to take care of my son, and for not being in a position yet again, to take care of myself.

As I saw myself surely beginning to slide down the slippery slope, I tried grasping for any and all of the tools I had been taught, but none of them seemed strong enough to hold me. Until I realized what was actually inside me, what didn't need any external confirmation or proof - the joy that enlarged MY heart - the little (ok, big) miracle that lay under the best medical care, improving day by day, just as I was. It was at that point that I realized not even miles and miles of concrete or time apart could break our connection.

It was remembering that I had a choice on how I could see our situation; as victims or as victors. Because this birth seemed almost worse than the first, my mind and my expectations went directly to how I responded the first time around - which opened the door with a flourish for postpartum to waltz right through and claim me as its dancing partner. But I decided that too much dancing wore me out and made me dizzy the last time, and I chose to be more present, more aware; more in awe of the absolute miracle I had created and the unshakable joy I felt at being a mom again. And I remember clearly, as if it were yesterday, the day we were able to bring you home; how green and lush and full of life everything was - as if pushed and pulled from the earth just to celebrate your arrival, and our victory! And it was with a feeling of lightness instead of heaviness that I carried our second little man through the front door to meet his big brother. Fear as well, but it was a healthy fear and excitement for the unknown and unexpected, not the dread of what could be ahead of me - so much different than the first time around.

I was much better prepared for the possibility of postpartum depression during my second pregnancy. I had done the work and knew the signs to look for so that with the help of my doctors, we could jump all over anything that had the potential to knock me off my center. No doubt we missed many of these signs as depression doesn't cater to what we want, it just looks for a crack to get in - the proverbial foot in the door. I think the true belief that I had a choice is what ultimately made the difference and gave me a different kind of strength. As I mentioned, the decision to be a victim or victor. But also the choice to acknowledge depression as part of who I am - part of my shadow.

Looking at it in this way allowed me to shine light into the darkness. It gave me strength in times where I thought weakness and despair were the only two options. It gave me the will to persevere and believe in my capabilities rather than wallow in my failures and shortcomings.

All told, it gave me the edge I needed, my own footholds, psychological building blocks I could use to get me through one day at a time. It was a long road back to a place where I felt good enough about myself and comfortable enough to confidently step into my full role as a mom, even though I had been doing a damned amazing job at being a mom already! It took a couple of years before I stepped back into my own power and had the strength to believe that I was more than capable of living my life on my terms. I worried (still do) whenever I felt/feel low that it might be the beginning of another slide into depression. I believed back then that I only had two courses of action – pretend everything was ok, or hide from the world until I felt I could pretend it was – I have done and still do a lot of hiding.

When I feel like there is an unspoken expectation that life is supposed to be light and bright, I wonder about the dull, blah days that I honestly experience. Some days, it was/is much easier to put on the mask and pretend that everything is the 'same ole, same ole' – especially when I can't figure out why I am feeling what I am feeling. With help, it has become easier to understand why I see my dark skies as abnormal, shameful or wrong. Each episode has given me insight into myself that is priceless. Depression isn't just waiting for a weak moment to "get me," but it is something that has taught me to be mindful of myself and my triggers. There are times when it has slipped up on me, and times when I knew I was slipping – but every time, it is a definite struggle of who and how to ask for help – too scared to trust, too proud to admit I need the help.

Experience is what has taught me that though the shadow is there, it is has become less and less frightening. It is so easy to slip behind the veil, and even easier to hide behind it – easy to smile on the outside while drying up on the inside - not wanting to burden anyone else with my problems.

So many women think they must go through life with their stories locked inside them because fear and shame hold us back from living our fullest potential. We allow what we think society has already decided for us to define us, instead of taking action for ourselves or at least talking to or asking for help from people who we know we are safe to share with. The fear of failure, of judgement, is a powerful factor that held me back from voicing what I was going through.

I could not fathom that the woman in front of me in line who seemed to have it all together, might possibly have actually escaped her own house, just like me, to get OUT for any reason. Before her own demons and shame swallowed her up. Trying to deal with the guilt of needing to get away from her environment - just to feel if she is real for a few minutes. And the shame of feeling like a failure for having to leave to find a tiny moment of sanity. It never entered my mind that she could possibly be looking at me in the exact way I was looking at her.

With help from both friends and professionals, as well as the work I have done for myself, I have been able to dig through some of the sludge to find that the common denominator that lies beneath the layers and layers is the idea that I am wrong somehow. Wrong for wanting help, wrong for needing help, and this feeling is so strong and unrelenting because what lies beneath it is the feeling that I am useless. Sometimes it is tough to let go of who you thought you were, of who you thought you should be, who others thought you should be. Sometimes it seemed like this version of myself was the only option available. I didn't know what I didn't know; I was just doing my best to survive.

It is a constant process, but so is life. And each time I feel more equipped to pull myself up and out. Gratitude and courage have taught me that no matter where I find myself, there is somewhere else I can be, and that I am strong enough and worthy enough to be there! The mental toll of depression doesn't ever seem to leave. It hides, it disguises itself, it goes dormant, but I feel that it is always there, somewhere under the surface; which is why I am grateful for what the experiences have taught me. I did not want what I was, where I was or who I was – this was not the life I thought I was supposed to have, that I felt I was entitled to. I was never promised an easy road, a beautiful landscape, or a predictable future, yet here I was stuck in what I didn't have instead of realizing what I did.

Words of wisdom once said to me were, "don't travel alone, it's not healthy." How many of us know this to be true, and yet do it anyway? I can only speak for myself, but I know my journey with depression has been one of painful, self-imposed solitude. It is not easy to share what I go through when people are used to seeing me as who I really am at my core – a happy, grateful, compassionate person who genuinely wants others to be happy as well.

Depression carries around with it some kind of badge of shame - I have heard from both people I knew were insensitive, but also those I thought were both sensitive and compassionate "I've been through (insert number) pregnancies, everyone gets tired and wrung out, so what's the big deal?" Well, that right there is actually the big deal - that those of us who do suffer from this medical condition feel incredibly guilty. Pile that on top of all the other negatives, and it is pretty hard to crawl out from under. So, when I do struggle, I tend to close up, go quiet, and put on a happy face when I am around others. I do not want to drag anyone into what I am going through, I do not want to bother or drag them down to where I really am. There is a whole myriad of feelings I have about myself, about how others will perceive me, about how I should be able to control this. But I know I can't. What I have learned is that I am still normal and that my struggles do not define who I am, that they are only a part of who I am.

The first step is always the hardest, but the one step of not judging myself against others, of realizing that every circumstance is relative to MY life gave me the courage to change my perspective. This doesn't mean my life is rosy, far from it, but no matter where I am, the first step is counting my blessings, then my accomplishments, then checking in with someone I trust – be it a friend, my doctor or my energy/life coach – and even my journal to see how far I have come and how I have been able to handle situations that came up in the past. There will always be trip wires that I may miss.

There may be days that I want to lie low because I am actually feeling low. And I know for sure there will be days that the feeling of less than will be overwhelming, and I will likely slip and fall. But knowing I am not alone, that what I am going through is not because I am wrong or bad or useless has diminished the strength of the grip depression has on me. I believe it will always be a part of me that I cannot completely get rid of, but if I can befriend it, hold space for it, and know that I have the tools I need to deal with it. I know that I will always have the courage to change from where I find my present self to where I want to be.

To think twenty years have passed seems like an eternity, and yet it is as fresh in my mind (and in my body sometimes) as if it happened yesterday. I don't think I will ever shake how it felt, I wonder all the time if things would have been different if I had been diagnosed and treated earlier. While I do not wish anyone to have gone through postpartum depression, I am grateful for what it has taught me; that I am strong, I am resilient, and that even though I may need help, I am still unbelievably amazing! I do not wear my depression as a badge of honour, I wear it as a badge of courage. Courage to see it, the courage to feel it, the courage to choose my way out each and every day.

LIFE AFTER
BETRAYAL

The Courage to Change

Daniella Hines

Daniella was born in the Durham Region just east of Toronto and has made her home there with her three beautiful children. However, she considers herself a global citizen after having had the opportunity to live and work all over the planet.

Early in life, she started on the life plan she made for herself at the age of 16 by completing a very practical commerce degree. She then started an educational travel business with her husband, which allowed for many grand journeys (though they all paled in comparison to the adventures in parenting).

In pursuit of finding her bliss, she followed her plan by getting married, having kids, finding a well-paid job and buying a nice house. Completing what she incorrectly believed was her purpose by her mid-thirties left her feeling unfulfilled and uncertain about what to do next. The universe swiftly shook things up to allow for more. She shed her husband and first business to start fresh in the worlds of yoga and personal development as a life coach, laughter yoga instructor, children's yoga teacher and reiki master.

Her journey has taken her from having one lifelong sexual partner to the beautiful buffet life has to offer. Her path has allowed her to taste the rainbows of life and ride the waves of fear and depression to find herself, her place and her mission. She is now focused on building her in-home Whitby yoga studio and reiki retreat while continuing her mission of growth and awakening.

Daniella's passion of helping women find their way back to wholeness is clear through her coaching, yoga and reiki services provided both online and in person. You can find Daniella, her current projects, blogs and schedules through her website www.daniellahines.com.

The Path Back to Me
by Daniella Hines

On my sixth Mother's Day, after putting my children to bed, I saw a text on my husband's phone that forever changed me.

My mind cleared, and a calm unlike anything I had ever experienced entered my body. I became laser-focused. He was standing eight feet away from me, and I could feel the fearful anxiety burst from his body.

I asked him about the text.

When I first signed up to participate in writing a chapter for this book, I was in a place of internal power. I had just decided I would be a life coach and I was ready to take on the world. I was in the kind of expansive state experienced when I'm sitting securely in my truth and fully self-aware. My awakening has been a deliberate but dramatic rollercoaster from self-loathing to overwhelming self-love and pride. And sometimes the ride takes me for full-on amusement style loops of bat-shit crazy.

I want this chapter to tell my story by sharing my struggles and successes, by allowing me to be part of something bigger than myself and by showing there are so many ways to achieve happiness. However, shortly after agreeing to contribute to this book, I once again fell asleep at the wheel of my life.

One of the biggest fears I had when deciding to join with these amazing women and write a chapter was letting my dirty laundry be seen. But as my editor so strongly told me: I cannot write with *my mother* as my editor. I must write my truth for myself and for women like me. So, in the same way that Brené Brown says it's only through vulnerability that we grow – here goes.

My ex-husband and I decided that our living arrangement had to change ASAP before one of us was found buried in the backyard. This book was shoved onto the backburner once my fear and worthiness issues were triggered. Every time I thought about writing, I just froze — like, full-on statue froze. I was passively waiting for the mood to write to strike me, all while avoiding my computer, to the point of losing the power cord of my laptop. Between cleaning a house cluttered by a year of depressed neglect and three hoarding children, I tried to rally my inner strength to just get started. The disappointment in myself built up relentlessly, and I began to experience disappointment in myself for the resurfacing of bad habits I thought I'd dropped. My yoga and meditation practice fell off. I even stopped washing my face at night. That's when I realized I was in a shit-or-get-off-the-pot situation.

So here is my shit.

After a few minutes of my husband trying to convince me I hadn't actually seen any text at all, my calmness softened him. He began to tell me his story. He didn't share all his truths, but he said enough to paint a picture of deception and lies, of places and women and things that an hour before were completely beyond my most fear-filled nightmares. The rage crept in as I looked at his crestfallen face, sensing in my core that his regret was at being caught and not about the pain that this revelation would cause for our family.

At this point in my life, I blatantly ignored all my intuition. I was entirely reactionary and not in touch with the deeper feelings that lay beneath the rage that flowed from me. I lost myself in despair and self-loathing. I instantly took on responsibility, shame and blame for causing him to need other women – for never being enough. As I attacked him verbally, I saved the cruellest words and feelings for myself. My thoughts went to: *Is he going to leave me now? Can I fix this so that he won't break up our family? How could I have let myself get so fat — of course he wants someone else.* My default was to berate myself and fuel the self-hatred I had so fully embraced.

I look back today with so much compassion for the woman I was, the sadness that consumed me and the way I dealt with the situation.

If I didn't value myself, why would he?

I never felt any shame or negative emotions around being raised in a non-traditional family. The only thing that stayed with me was a wish for it to be easier, so I wouldn't have to explain myself or hide anything from the outside world.

I was raised by my mother and her partner until I was 16. I didn't have any sense of my family being different until I was about eight years old, though I didn't really think anything of it. The 80's weren't an accepting time for gay marriage or child rearing so, until high school, we all kept it a secret. As far as other people knew, the spare room was for my mom's friend.

I became an expert liar at a young age. Though I didn't ever fully understand why we needed to lie, I never questioned it as a child.

We lied a lot in my home. When my grandparents would ask how much things cost, the answer was never more than half of the real price. We never talked about mom's partner's mental health or if she was on or off her lithium, drinking or sober. We were smooth and happy for all those around us. My mom took pride in how we appeared to other people. I shared that pride and loved when my mother dressed me up so that the extended family would gush about how cute I was. I brought joy to my mom's world and I was thrilled about it.

Outside of the house, I smiled every day. Every single day, no matter what was going on inside. That's how I was taught to live, so that's what I did for 37 years. I like to smile. It helps others to feel at ease. When people are at ease, they don't ask deep questions. I didn't ask deep questions either. I existed on the surface layer of my feelings, while I shoved the anger, resentment and disappointments deep down inside of me. If they surfaced, as they did every now and again, I would find someplace to be alone, scream and rage and sob until the feelings were gone, and then I'd pick myself up again.

I had the picture-perfect life — a husband who (I thought) adored me, a mother that was always around, beautiful children, a gorgeous home, a business that allowed for amazing travel and paid all the bills. But I wasn't happy and I hated myself for not being able to just be grateful for everything I had. I mean, I had it good, didn't I? My husband cleaned the kitchen without me having to ask, I had no debt and my kids were overall easy to parent. C'mon, I had the life that everyone dreamed of, right? But no one knew that every day I was struggling with myself — eating candies that I'd hidden in my closet, pretending to go to the gym so that I could go to McDonald's, eat Egg McMuffins and stream TV shows on my phone.

I was a miserable mess.

My entire life had revolved around him since I was sixteen years old — from the friends I kept, to the university I attended and to the business we ran together. He was the interesting one, the passionate one, and I was the wind beneath his wings. But now, I didn't want to be that for him anymore. I became so consumed by all the things that were happening in our lives that I lost focus on my husband and I as a couple. I threw myself into motherhood and the challenge of loving/surviving our three kids. I disengaged from our family business and started a direct sales part-time gig that brought many amazing women into my life.

I had started to shift my life away from his. I did not do this consciously, but in retrospect I can see now that I began to pull away and find my strengths. I found small joys in my successes outside of him and the business we'd built together. I was discovering through my side business that people liked me, without him. I found out that I had value beyond just being someone's wife and mother.

For two years, we stayed the course and played house together. We danced around our obvious unhappiness, surviving every day but never living. I didn't know how to stay in my newfound power, so I fell into a cycle of affirming my inner strength then spiralling into worthlessness and despair, fuelled by fear that people would discover I was a fraud that needed him to pick up my pieces. I have very few memories of us as a couple from this time. Yet the thought of leaving never once occurred to me. I would have stayed in the half-living forever, rushing bedtime with my children so I could get to the couch, numb out and consume comforting calories as I watched shows about other people living great lives.

Then we travelled to South Africa, which turned out to be our final business trip together.

We had finally reached the point we had always talked about, when we could take our children on the conservation biology trips our business ran for school groups. This had been our dream for years. We would be the amazing parents that would raise global children. We had a trip that looked near-perfect on social media. I even ran my side business from South Africa and had my highest team sales yet. But the reality behind the Facebook posts was a completely different story. We lost car seats somewhere between bush camp and the dive site. Our youngest child was still in diapers and finding ways to manage an active, strong-willed little boy in that environment was extremely challenging. One camp had deadly scorpions and spitting cobras, and our oldest child was fascinated. My daughter's gluten and dairy intolerances made for a challenging fourth birthday in the bush. Thank goodness, the rangers figured out how to make a gluten free cake!

The dream of doing it all together had a very different reality, as my husband was working solidly and not participating in any family time while I was consumed with the children; not able to work at all. This is the point where I should mention that, on top of everything else, we were responsible for 50 sixteen-year-olds. I look back and can only laugh and be thankful that we all made it through, but at the time, my stress levels were through the roof. Maintaining the look of perfection was very overwhelming.

Once we got home, barely on speaking terms, my husband confronted me with his issues around intimacy in our marriage. Up until this point our sex life was all about him. Through no fault of his own, I simply had no interest. I would feel the urges but years of built-up layers of resentment and disappointment had blocked me from bringing them to my husband. We had what I assumed was regular marital sex, that was more than what most of my friends were having, so I felt like I was doing my job. This concept makes me cringe today.

Looking back, after having now taken the time to discover my sexuality and find my sex drive, I feel a lot of remorse about that part of my marriage.

At 39 years old, I enjoyed my second man. This sentence brings me girlish joy to say.

I was still married but had been presented with an ultimatum by my husband that we open our marriage or it was over. I was devastated. I had never slept with another man and although my issues around his infidelity were focused on how we felt about the situation and not the actual physical act, the idea felt extreme to me. After an epic battle that left me wondering how on earth I was married to a man so oblivious to me, I left the house for a four-day hotel escape that would forever change the trajectory of my life.

On my second night in the hotel, away from him and my children, I tried to come to terms with this new lifestyle. I opened up to my marriage counsellor and her advice was: "Your marriage is either over or you can give what he is proposing a try. Worst case your marriage ends but what if ..."

So, on night three of my hotel escape, I opened a Tinder account. I was admittedly not sober; however, I was completely confident that this was what I wanted. I let go of all my thoughts about my marriage and what this step could mean. I was much too scared to put a picture of my face online. What if my neighbours or friends saw my profile? I took 80 pictures of my neck in the hotel bathroom. The profile took me three hours to create — I started and deleted it a million times. I had absolutely no idea what to say about myself. Did I have to say I was fat? I didn't want anyone showing up and seeing the size of my ass and leaving. A nice word for fat is "curvy," so yes — that was going in for sure. I decided to mention my open marriage. I needed to say it out loud and write it down to make it real.

How do you say politely: *I just want to have sex, maybe a few times but nothing more*? I hated that anyone would think I was using them, though I had yet to comprehend the differences in male versus female brains.

Once my Tinder profile was complete, I took the tutorial on how to use the app and started swiping. Instantly, I realized I didn't have to be with men like my husband, and started to notice a pattern in my desires. This was the first time I thought about what turns me on, about what appeals to me. One of the first things I realized is that I wanted a big man. Beards really appealed to me. I loved the fun bios that had personality — I read every one.

I started to get matches. A LOT of matches. They liked me! It was exhilarating. I talked to 20+ men that night, but one was replying more quickly to everything I said. So, I jumped in and set up a date for the next day.

I decided not to bother with pretence. I met him in my hotel lobby. I look back and am in awe of how beautifully I fell into confidence, into the conviction and power I felt. I was sexy, desirable, ready for anything. I was in control. It was crazy. I completely forgot I was a fat soccer mom from the suburbs — the negative self-talk went quiet. I was the owner of my life. For the first time, I wasn't thinking of anyone else's needs or ideas about what I should be doing or what I should look like. This was the real me, the me that could be anything and do anything I desired. It was my first taste of freedom; it was my first venture into self-discovery.

He walked into the lobby, and he was beautiful. I could see the bulge of his bicep in his coat and his bald black scalp reflected the ceiling lights like he was the sky full of stars. He hugged me and I could feel how hard his body was. My head nestled into his Tide-scented shoulder and I felt like I was in another universe. He said hello as his chiseled face and thick soft lips smiled. He stuttered that it was nice to meet me. His stutter and obvious nerves gave me even more energy. Had I ever felt this burn inside my body before? I was a sexy goddess and I was going to fulfill my every desire. We talked for maybe ten minutes before I could no longer control my need to kiss him. I took his hand gently, then firmly directed him to my room. Who the hell was this woman, I kept asking myself, because I could never have done this two days ago. I would have been in shock about the stupidity of it and all the ways it could go horribly wrong. But it didn't. It played out just like those Harlequin novels you used to pick up in the supermarket checkout line.

My husband and I created rule upon rule on how we would navigate an open marriage. He had read many books and clearly had been planning it out for some time. None of it worked out as intended and I was continuously disappointed and fearful of losing him. Then, on his second date with another woman, he fell in love. Opening the marriage had led to the end of the marriage. It was an ugly, drawn out, push-pull of love and power that left me face down in the mud. To add insult to injury, he took her on our trip to the Galapagos instead of me.

To say that I was lost without him is an epic understatement. Since the age of 16 he had been the main consideration in every decision I made in my life. It was like I had half my brain and heart cut out. I was filled with self-loathing and resentment — all the negative feelings in existence.

I began to hunt for new forms of validation. One of the paths was back to Tinder.

Over the ensuing twelve months I fell in and out of love many times, sometimes for only a few hours. Every date gave me hope that my white knight would appear and save me from my life. I tried on so many personas to find one that fit. I worked to become the dream woman for men that was completely open to discovering what they loved. The men I met through Tinder gave me the space to work though those possibilities.

At my core, I am deeply loving and I find joy in building others up emotionally. This manifested as the first persona I tried on for size. I desperately wanted to be loved and acknowledged for all I was trying to be for them. I was entirely focused on ego stroking. No matter how I was touched I would praise them. No matter what they offered to me I strove to find joy in it, to be in love with it. This led me to many months without experiencing orgasm and I struggled to fit into the boxes they built for me. Looking back, I can see that this was who I was for my husband. I desperately tried to be what he wanted me to be while having no idea who I actually was. The resentment of not being seen eventually became more than either of us could bear. I could never give him my 50% to create a whole within our marriage. I never revealed myself to him. I didn't know who I was so I couldn't even begin to try.

The personas came and went in rapid succession, like items crossed off a grocery list. I couldn't permit myself to submit to a man's complete will. One man would bite me during orgasm and my gut reaction was to punch him in the face, not to endure or enjoy. I couldn't dominate or degrade or speak cruel words another man asked for me to say. It hurt my soul to say such things. A night on the town with a man in drag was fun as hell but it was a love of sharing openness that appealed. Undressing him at the end of the night was entirely for his pleasure, as I felt no heat or arousal. Through this process, I slowly discovered that deep love of sharing and complete openness could be friendship. That's the way I want to live — with complete openness to the choices of those who I enjoy having in my life. But love and relationship had to bring me the same burn I was giving to my partners. That, I discovered, was non-negotiable.

Searching for what I needed swung the other way. I ultimately tried on my princess — allowing myself to be the center of a relationship, the object of desire, giving only what felt good for me in each moment. I permitted myself to believe that allowing a man to be my saviour, to be my white knight, would fulfill us both. Unfortunately, this did not turn out as planned. I could no longer live in a box and I had to reclaim my freedom.

Upon reflection, I can see now that I was giving away all of myself, without realizing that what I needed was to focus internally, which was something I had never done in my life. I stopped pretending to orgasm to soothe the sexual egos of men. I began to make them work for it, allowing us both to learn from the experience. I discovered different types of orgasms and how to bring my body to unbelievable heights. I opened my mind with fascination to how fetishes develop, letting go of all judgements in the process. I found pleasure in things I had never heard of, loving the learning from people with passion. I opened all of myself to each experience.

I was slowly discovering what I wanted sexually and who I really was as opposed to what was expected of me. I reached the conclusion that I was a very sexual being, which was a very different reality to the one my marriage had constructed for me. I felt like I finally had a truer understanding of my sexual needs and the ways men and women are fundamentally different.

This realization helped me significantly in my understanding of some of my husband's motivations and reactions. It allowed me to let go of my anger and own my role in our problems. I used this time to ask questions and have meaningful conversations with men in order to connect as much as they would allow. I practiced having an open heart and permitting myself to be fully present as I lived each moment. I focused away from my day-to-day life to begin to see what feeling everything and being open could look like. This awareness and awakening did not translate into my real life right away.

Outside of those moments when I returned to my day-to-day life with my ex-husband in our matrimonial home, I cried, raged and begged the universe to not be so hard on me. I saw myself as a victim of life in which my less-than-idyllic childhood had left me vulnerable to becoming dependent on my ex for everything. Now I was alone. I didn't know how to be on my own and fully responsible for myself. I noticed that I was overwhelmed by almost everything, even the simple task of replacing a lightbulb, yet I never knew what would set me off in tears or a rage. My desire to overcome my anxiety led me to become medicated. I struggled for five months before accepting that I needed the help I'm so grateful I finally got from my doctor.

I just didn't want to be in the driver's seat of life. It turns out that avoiding the task of taking the wheel had been my default mode my whole life. I continued to wait for my white knight to rescue me and allow the open, sexy, strong woman that I portrayed on Tinder to meld with the rest of my world.

In my early twenties while on a trip to New York City, I walked into a Tiffany's for the first time. It dazzled me and I just HAD to buy myself something. I was a poor newlywed so there were very few things I could even consider, but I found a cursive "d" silver necklace. It cost $125, well beyond what I should have been spending on myself, as I had nothing but dreams in my pocket. But it called out to me with a loud need.

A few months later, having put in on backwards, I accidentally had a "b" and not a "d" around my neck. While deep into a fight with my husband, he noticed the "b" and said I'd switched over into bitch mode. I was infuriated, yet somehow it became a norm between us.

The B became Barbra, my alter ego.

It was only while on my path of self-discovery after my separation that I acknowledged Barbra for who she was for me. She was my inner voice that took no shit, and raged against those that slighted me. She was my defender and my call to action, yet at the same time, she was also the one who kept me small.

For me, the ultimate tell that she is taking over comes through eating. Barbra is in control when my attention is no longer on how food will feel in my body or how it will nourish me and show my body love. Barbra is in the building when I'm no longer conscious of my choices and I finish all the kids' leftover Easter eggs or open the Girl Guide cookies because I was going to let them have some tomorrow anyway, right? When I stopped asking myself why I wanted the treat, Barbra has silenced my inner voice.

The key has been just that — asking why if I can't find an answer. It's then that I need meditation instead of food. It has been in the asking of the questions that I've found trust in myself. I used to think that once I had this figured out I was going to be golden. But Barbra still takes over because she's a hardcore bitch. She can pack a whole house in just a few weeks while managing three kids, a business and various other obligations. She doesn't have time to meditate. Fuck that. She doesn't care about health, or about tomorrow — just about how to function today, right now. She loves chocolate and long Netflix binge sessions. Her only focus is on getting shit done and finding pleasure. I can usually see when she has taken over.

Sometimes I'm days in before I wake up from the Barbra trance. I am not militant in my eating — I want to live a balanced life, so a single slice of birthday cake with ice cream must be part of it. When the consumption is not questioned and the quantity not noticed, Barbra is here or pushing to take over.

Through therapy and hours of journaling, I have learned to accept Barbra. I've become aware that if I avoid letting her take over I can conquer my negative feelings. Each time I go through a difficult emotional period, the process takes less and less out of me. It was in this way that I started to gain more trust in myself. I know that I am strong enough to face the world with an open heart and capable of sharing my light and love with others, in part because of what Barbra has taught me.

Along the way, I found yoga.

I discovered that I loved people that do yoga. They see the world in a different light than I had ever considered. I became curious about how they live in their open hearts and minds consistently. I had learned to open myself fully in the bedroom behind the safety of walls and covers, but I wanted to learn to live fully open every day. Yoga was not just stretching and exercise, as I had previously assumed. It was a way of life, a philosophy of being. I had no idea where it would lead me but I had to find another path to heal.

I enrolled in a 40-day program at my studio, which included yoga six times a week and daily meditation that increased in duration each week. It was the deep questions from each chapter of our guide that created the biggest shift. It was a shift of personal accountability. I realized that I wasn't living a full life. I didn't enjoy looking inward but when I did, and I stayed in the fire of self-doubt and worthlessness, I could see and feel that I was more. I held a limiting belief that I was lazy. I started to pay closer attention to what motivated me. I realized that my procrastination was often about resistance! As I began to incorporate practices that I loved into my daily life, like yoga and reiki, I began to see I was not lazy at all. Looking back now, I can see that having three kids, running two businesses while also maintaining many personal relationships can't be lazy.

Perspective shifts began to change, not only how I saw myself, but how I viewed the world. I started to become fascinated with *me*. I signed up to do all kinds of classes. I love the learning and the investment I've made in myself. I opened up to the universe and became a *yes* in my life.

M.J. Wilson

In 2009, after years spent in a difficult marriage, M.J found the courage to walk away. She became a single mom to four wonderful kids and started the unexpected journey of finding herself.

She worked for over 20 years in the childcare industry before deciding to go back to school to be trained as a family mediator. She now spends her days navigating a second marriage, while perfecting the art of being a mom and step-mom. In her spare time, she is extremely passionate about encouraging women to Move Beyond Their Divorce.

M.J helps women break free from the usual divorce traps and teaches them how to not get stuck in the negative that often surrounds it. She can occasionally be found writing blog posts for Move Beyond Divorce Coaching, encouraging women and men to live their best life after divorce.

Hearing My Own Heart
by M.J. Wilson

Deciding to leave my husband was one of the hardest and yet easiest, decisions I ever made. I'm not supposed to admit to the easy part, but it's true. After almost sixteen years together, thirteen and a half of those married, I was done. Completely and totally done. No turning back, no second guessing, no maybe, no what-ifs. Just completely and totally, finished. The night he left, was like a weight was lifted off me and I slept soundly for the first time in years. I spent all that summer waiting. Waiting to feel regret. Waiting to ask him to come back. Waiting for my kids to beg me to put our family back together. None of that happened. In fact, none of it even came close to happening. None of my children had meltdowns. None of them even really questioned why we were no longer together. It was like somehow, they knew. Somehow us splitting up brought peace into our lives.

Looking back, I knew he was wrong for me. I knew that I should have walked away long before anything really got started. There were so many warning signs, so many things that I just ignored. It's amazing how many people came out of the woodwork to give me their opinions when I finally called it quits. None of those opinions were good. None suggested I'd made the right choice so many years ago. Most were just so thankful that I'd finally made the decision I made then...the decision to walk away.

I was raised in a strict, Christian home, the middle of three kids. I have an older brother and a younger sister, and I suffer entirely from middle sibling syndrome. My dad was a pastor and church planter, while my mother ran an in-home daycare. This meant that for most of my childhood, we were either starting churches from scratch or trying to keep a small church alive and growing, all while having a house full of other people's kids. We grew up in what would be considered a lower income family and I started working and earning my own money around the age of eleven. I know my parents loved us and did the best they could, given the decisions they made about their paths and goals in life.

There were very few times I was ever resentful of my childhood and despite the lack of money, my childhood was happy. We were always surrounded by family friends, that loved us and were interested in us. I grew up with wonderful Christian mentors, women who loved God, church and the men they were married to. I was also surrounded by men, who were great examples of how a husband should treat their wives and provide for their families. From as far back as I can remember, this is what I wanted. I wanted to get married to a man who loved God and his family and would do anything for me. I wanted to stay at home and have babies. I didn't care if I got an education because being a wife and a mother was my only dream.

Looking back, I don't think I came to this dream all on my own. I think I was carefully, if unconsciously, nudged into it. I was moulded from a very young age to aspire to this and nothing more. My parents took my love of kids and ran with it. I still remember the feelings of happiness that came with the idea that I would follow in their footsteps and be married at the age of nineteen. I was a people-pleaser, and this fulfilled my need to please them.

I struggled in school and I doubted my abilities when it came to anything academic. My self-doubt was affirmed at times, and I was left believing that the only way I would receive complete approval was if I was married young and had babies young. I excelled in anything child-related. I was a great camp counsellor, children loved being part of my Sunday School class, I taught swimming lessons for six years and babysat for dozens of families. Everywhere I went, children were drawn to me, and parents never worried when I was around. It was just assumed that if I did ever work, it would be with children. I learned at a very young age that my perfect answer to the question "what do you want to be when you grow up?" was a teacher. This answer would elicit a positive response every single time I said it, and it wasn't long before I truly believed my own answer.

My childhood was filled with mixed messages. Part of the reasoning behind getting married young was to prevent us kids from having any physical interaction with a potential boyfriend or girlfriend. This included almost all forms of physical contact. Sex before marriage was strictly forbidden and one of the worst sins you could possibly commit. I do believe my parents felt that by us marrying young, we would be saved from this temptation.

The whole time my parents were planting the seeds for young weddings, we were also being raised with the assumption that all of us would attend university. This was non-negotiable. I do believe, that this was not so we would have the education required for a specific job, but rather to have the prestige of saying we were university grads. Any attempt to protest this or suggest any other form of schooling was met with statistics letting us know how lucky we would be to have a university degree and how few people in Canada actually held such a thing.

Based on my upbringing, you can imagine my excitement when, come grade twelve, I found the man of my dreams. The one who was going to help fulfill my destiny. We had the most wonderful high school love story, and I was beyond excited at the thought that my life was taking the direction it was supposed to. This boy fit perfectly into my life. My parents loved him, my sister loved him, he attended church with us and soon became a permanent fixture in our home. He became everything I needed him to be, until one day he wasn't. Three weeks before we were to be married, my fiancé had a change of heart, and the wedding was called off. To add insult to injury, moments after having my wedding called off, I received rejection letters from every university I had applied to. I was devastated and felt like a failure. I had no backup plan, no direction for my life, no idea what to do. Soon after, my parents moved three hours away from me and I was left to figure out life, on my own, at the age of nineteen.

It was shortly after this I met my former husband. He came from a good family, had grown up attending church, had a university degree and helped coach my friend's son in hockey. This is how we met. The beginning of our relationship was exactly what I needed to help get over my high school love. I quickly fell in love with his family and spent as much time as possible with him and them. He was a few years older than me and I felt like the luckiest girl ever. Never would I have believed that someone like him, would fall for someone like me. I had no education, no money, nothing material to offer anyone. I was nice, that was it. That was all I had to offer any potential partner, and I was under the belief that it didn't always count for much.

Growing up in a Christian home meant that I spent my whole life being taught that once you are married, you are always married. I was raised to believe that getting divorced was one of the greatest sins you can commit as an adult. I spent over twenty years attending church, and I have zero memories of ever being taught when it was okay to leave a marriage.

When I had been married to my first husband for two months, he started having an affair with an old girlfriend. After screaming and crying and feeling like a complete fool, I asked him to leave. I needed space, and he needed to decide who he wanted to be with... her or me. For eight months he continued this relationship, while I tried to pick up the pieces of my life. I found a good lawyer and attempted to take back some control of my life. I filed paperwork and started the divorce process-the entire time wondering how I could be such a complete failure and how I could have overlooked so many warning signs.

My entire life, I had been the nice, kind, forgiving one. I was the one in the family who never wanted anyone mad at them. I would go out of my way to make everyone around me happy. My father used to tell me how he would worry because one of my best traits was also the one that could cause me the most pain. When I was in middle school, I would forgive the girls that were the bullies and invite them over again and again. I was anyone and everyone's friend. I had a very forgiving nature and always tried to see the best in everyone. This trait played a huge role when the affair happened. I explained it away as only an expert could. I gave him every excuse as to why he did what he did. We were too young, he had unfinished business with his ex, he wasn't ready for the commitment. I made excuse after excuse, trying desperately to make sense of the unimaginable and find a reason to be able to forgive him.

After several months of living apart, his other relationship ended, and I was desperate to give things one more try. I felt like I owed it to both of us to not give up so quickly. I also felt like I could finally erase some of the shame I was believed to have brought on my family because of the split. We went to therapy and life returned to normal...sort of. See, the thing that no one ever tells you is that getting past an affair is an almost impossible task. It is not as easy as an apology or a few counselling sessions. The damage that is done is indescribable. The insecurity, the distrust, the loneliness, all of it, a terrible, gut wrenching pain that dims over time but never really goes out.

For thirteen and a half years, I tried to make it work between us. I tried so hard to forgive and forget. Funny thing is, I could forgive him, but I could never forget, and I could never trust him. I tried, I had children with him, went on vacation with him, bought a house with him and I overlooked so many warning signs that it was happening again. In my mind, the more time that went by the more I thought I didn't have a good reason to leave him. As each year passed and each baby was born, I truly felt that no one would understand why I needed to get out of my marriage.

So many family members and church members were thrilled that I made things work. I was repeatedly told how happy everyone was that we had worked things out. I was constantly made aware that it was the right thing to do. It was better for us and better for the children. As Christians, you don't divorce. You allow your spouse to treat you however they want, and you don't ever leave. I was a pastor's kid, and that made it even more important that I maintain the image of having been in a loving, forgiving marriage. I became so scared of what my family would think if I made the decision to leave. I was terrified I would never be forgiven for the sin of divorce, and I was afraid of being judged for the decision I so desperately wanted to make.

What the church forgets to teach you, is that you are God's temple and you are made in the image of Him. God did not make you to be abused in any sense of the word. He did not give you your body and your mind so that someone else could destroy it. God's purpose for you has always been to make you feel loved and worthy. Although adultery is one of the Ten Commandments, I still spent thirty-five years of my life thinking that I would go to Hell if I ever walked away from my marriage because of it.

For thirteen years, money had been an issue between us. My former husband was responsible for all our bills and I had very little knowledge regarding our finances. I had been raised never to question or talk about money. He was a financial planner and, in the beginning, I had complete trust in him and his abilities. It took me several years to realize just how wrong I was. During our marriage, my first husband mishandled our funds, borrowed thousands of dollars without my knowledge, racked up tens of thousands of dollars in debt behind my back, drained our children's education funds- all while accusing me of spending too much.

I worked hard throughout our entire marriage to make sure my kids had everything I never did. My kids were never spoiled, but they did enjoy many luxuries in life. There was a lot of resentment from both of us regarding the other person's perception of money and use of money, as well as what each of us considered a normal work week. My first husband was self-employed and worked from home. This meant I got to see how many hours he actually worked. Resentment began to grow inside of me, when I began to realize the truth of his work situation. For thirteen years, I worked upwards of twelve hours a day, never complaining, never taking a proper maternity leave, only taking vacation when it was something for our family, all while watching him work minimal hours. His pay was commission-based, and I never did understand why he would never put in the time needed to secure a proper pay cheque.

Our fights around his work and money grew more frequent, and it was just after our thirteenth wedding anniversary that my former husband tried to take his life. It was the week after Christmas, and he admitted to spending money that wasn't his to spend. Money that had been entrusted to him by local parents connected to my son's hockey team. It was during this week that I finally got the nerve to tell him I had had enough, and I was leaving. For the first time ever, I had found a potential house to move myself and my kids to. After so many years of stress and worry, I was finally prepared to give up everything I had worked so hard for. I was willing to say goodbye to my dream home, cottage visits, yearly holidays in Florida. For the first time ever, I thought I had reached my limit but, like so many times before, I started feeling sorry for him and convinced myself that with enough love and patience from me, things would change – he would change. Looking back, I now know that's not how it works. No amount of love and understanding from me would ever have been enough to change the core of who he was. He had been this way and had these traits his whole life. This is who he was.

It was during this week after Christmas that he seriously began plotting his attempted suicide. He started writing journal entries addressed to me, trying to explain why this was his only option. These entries were for me to find and read after his attempt had been carried out. Every journal entry started with a comment related to something I had said to him and ended with making sure I knew he was doing this because of what I had said. He tried to explain how this would take care of all our financial worries and how the kids and I would be set for a life without him. Every entry was pointed directly at me being the reason that this was the only solution. He was very calculating with his words, and there was the perfect amount of guilt in each and every entry.

His suicide attempt was to take place on what would turn out to be the coldest evening of January 2009. At this point, he had started delivering pizzas in the evenings, to make up for some of the income he was continuously losing by not working full-time during the day. He went to work as usual that evening, returning home sometime around or after midnight. He apparently kissed us all goodbye and left the house for what he thought would be the last time. He proceeded to park his car in a local parking lot and took a bottle of sleeping pills. He later stated that his intention was to then start the engine and have the exhaust come back into the car. Turns out, the car had never been started and the keys were not found in the ignition. This led police to wonder what his true intentions were.

Early the next morning, a police officer found him lying in the snow, suffering from extreme hypothermia. Two police officers arrived on my doorstep a few hours later. Unless you've had the unfortunate experience of watching a police officer walk up your front walk, holding your husband's license in their hand, you cannot even begin to imagine the feelings that rushed through me. I will forever be thankful to my best friend, who lived down the street and came to stay with me and the kids while I tried to locate him. I was able to meet the officers on my front step without any of my kids seeing. I attempted to remain composed knowing I had to go back inside. My girlfriend looked at me and, without saying a word, knew exactly what had happened. I had lived my entire married life with him continuously threatening to take his life; she knew he had finally tried.

I was driven to the hospital by one of the policewomen and escorted to my husband's side. At that moment, I became *that* woman. The woman no one wants to be. I was suddenly part of a club no one asks to join, and no one can ever leave. I was devastated, angry, and confused. No one could tell me if he would live. No one could tell me if he'd be okay if he did wake up. No one could tell me much of anything. I had no idea how I should feel or how I was supposed to act. The Christian in me told me to sit quietly by his side like the dutiful wife the church expected me to be. The hurt, betrayed part of me was screaming that it was all too much.

My ex-husband did wake up and did regain all function and memory. I got some tears from him and an apology. Unfortunately for him, I was familiar with the tears, and the apologies, and neither held much weight with me. My life was forever changed that day. I now spent every day worried that my husband would either be unfaithful, careless with money or would attempt to take his life again. I had been working full-time and had to scale back in order to be there for him. I pushed him to get help and seek counselling. Every attempt I made received pushback from him. He told me he was fine and that he just made a stupid mistake. His life continued as though nothing had ever happened. My life continued as if a huge boulder had been attached to my leg, and I was forced to drag it around with me every minute of every day. To this very day, he still has no real understanding of how much this impacted the rest of us.

I remember sitting in the hospital at his bedside, waiting for him to wake up and asking the ICU nurse what spouses usually did in this situation. Did they stay? Did they leave? Were they upset? Were they angry? I was in the midst of trying to navigate something I had no experience with, and I was really struggling. I will never forget her telling me that most spouses don't show up. They are angry and hurt, and want no part of what their spouse had attempted. For some weird reason, her response sparked some sort of heroic feeling in me and I remember thinking, "Wow, I'm among the few that show up." My family and his family rallied around him and gave him the support he felt he didn't need. At no point did he express any real remorse for what he had done or any thankfulness for what everyone did for him.

It was two months after his suicide attempt that I started seeing a Christian therapist. I was struggling and needed help. The weight of everything I had been through was becoming too much. In the weeks leading up to my ex-husband's attempt, I had prayed for a sign. I needed a sign to help show me if I should be staying or if I should be going. When he made the attempt on his life, I took that as a sign that I had to stay. There was no way I could leave him; he needed me. The problem was, staying was becoming suffocating. I couldn't breathe in our marriage, and it was slowly destroying me. Very few people knew the truth, I had become so good at wearing that smile and playing the role of the happy wife. I was hoping that by talking to a Christian therapist, I would be given some clarity on what I should be doing. I needed to know what the Bible said about my situation. Would my leaving be the great sin I had been raised to believe it would be? This therapist would help me understand that God never intended for us to live the life I was being forced to live. I credit her with changing my perspective of God's love and His grace and what it all means. She was the first person to let me know that it was okay if I said enough, that I would not be condemned to a life in hell, if I said no more. Ultimately, she gave me permission to walk away and save myself.

It took another two months for me to get the nerve to tell my ex-husband that I was done, that his suicide attempt was too much weight for me to carry. He didn't believe that it was over. He apologized again and swore his actions would never be repeated, that he had learned his lesson. Two months later, he moved out of our marital home, and within a few weeks, he was speaking to the woman who would eventually become his second wife.

My life changed in ways I would never have expected. The day my ex-husband moved out was the day I got my life back. It was also the day I could finally breathe again. The weight I had been continuously carrying around, slowly started to melt away. This does not mean that my life was suddenly easy. I was now a single mother of four kids all under the age of twelve. I was the one responsible for every aspect of their lives. Several of my kids have medical issues – Tourette's syndrome, autism, asthma, and an enzyme disorder. I have spent countless hours at doctor's appointments, at specialized clinics in hospitals, and in waiting rooms while my kids attend therapy. Three of my kids have IEPs at school. This means extra meetings at school, additional phone calls, and numerous emails. All of these have been done alone. The moment my ex-husband left was the moment he stopped being an active part of our children's lives.

He moved out July 6th, three days after my son's tenth birthday. He also chose to move out while my sister and her family were visiting us from out of town. During this time, I requested a meeting with the wife of our pastor. At the time, I felt an immense need to have her understanding of what I had experienced throughout my married life and her support in my decision to finally say, "Enough." She agreed to meet me at a local diner in town a few weeks after my ex-husband had moved out. When I arrived, she greeted me and explained she had brought her husband along because he had more experience with these issues. I spent the next hour and a half being made to feel incredibly small. As it turned out, the wife said almost nothing, and the pastor had very little understanding or compassion for what I had been through. I left that meeting swearing that I would never step foot inside that church again. How dare he criticize something he knew nothing about? He had no personal understanding of the weight adultery causes in a marriage. He had no idea what thirteen years of zero trust does to the relationship. That day, I made the decision to no longer allow him to pastor myself or my children.

That was also the day I lost faith in churches. I didn't lose faith in what I believe, that has never wavered, but I did lose confidence in the church's ability to handle divorce with grace. I lost faith in the church leader's ability to listen without judgement and to love unconditionally. All I wanted was for that pastor's wife to put her arms around me and tell me it was going to be okay. To tell me she understood. To tell me she would pray for myself and my children. Instead, she sat there while her husband, the leader of my church, told me I was wrong. That was the day I no longer cared what the church thought because they no longer cared about me.

My faith is stronger now, than it has ever been. I have surrounded myself with women who love God and share the same beliefs as I do. I have learned that you do not need a church building to learn about the love and forgiveness of God.

Something happened to me during the summer of 2009. Something changed in me and I finally found my courage and my voice. Something that had been brewing for thirteen years finally boiled over and I wasn't afraid anymore. I wasn't afraid to stand up for myself and my children. I wasn't afraid to fight for what I knew was true. That scared little girl, who was so eager to please everyone, finally said, "Enough."

That January, I moved my four kids and I, along with our two cats and my business, into a little three-bedroom home. I packed up every belonging we had and prepared to start all over again. I will forever be grateful to my friends and family who supported me during this time. To the ones who helped pack and unpack boxes with me. To the ones who took my middle-of-the-night phone calls. To the friends and family who never once told me I was doing the wrong thing. It was during this time that I learned who some of my true friends were-the ones who loved my children and me so unconditionally, they were never afraid of hurting the other side. Divorce has a funny way of dividing people and asking them to pick sides, as wrong as this is, I am so thankful to those who picked my side.

A few months after the kids and I moved, my ex-husband and I started mediation. In the beginning, it went well; we agreed on most things. When it came time to file the paperwork with the court, he changed his mind. Half the paperwork was filed, but he refused to file the rest of his forms. One thing I would not budge on was having sole custody of my children. It isn't granted very often but, in our case, and with his suicide attempt hardly in the past, I was not willing to take any chances with his mental state and my kids. Without funds to pay for a lawyer, I had to figure things out on my own. I became a regular at that courthouse. I would ask questions, talk to the free lawyer, the mediator, pretty much anyone who would listen. I will never forget the day, after speaking to several different people within the court system, I happened upon a clerk who thought he had a solution for me. He made no promise but felt his suggestion was worth a try. The papers granting me sole custody and granting our divorce came in the mail a few weeks later.

The day those papers arrived, was the beginning of my new life. It hasn't always been easy; we've been back to court several times and fought over several issues, but my life is now *my* life. Every hardship I endured those first few years of being separated and divorced, were worth every free breath I took then, and I take now. I now know myself better than I ever thought possible. I am strong and stubborn and worth so much more than I was ever made to believe. I am still the kind and gentle person I have always been, but I am also a fighter. I no longer care that people don't like me because how they feel is not a reflection of who I am.

I always assumed I would stay with my first husband until I was forty. I figured if I stayed until then, it would lessen people's upset with me. I had a plan, one I thought would make everyone else happy. At no point though did I ever put myself or my children first in this plan. I put my parents first, I put the church first, I put my misguided beliefs first, but never me. I will forever be grateful to my therapist, to my sister, to my cousin and to my friends, everyone who helped me see that, at thirty-five years of age, it was time to put *me* first. It was time for me to save myself and my children from his destructive behaviour. These women and men picked me up on days I felt I would break from the weight of it all. Never will I be able to repay all they have done. They have given me time I cannot possibly return. I am so very grateful for every single person God placed in my life while going through this. He knew exactly who I needed and blessed them with the words I needed to hear.

Since my divorce, I have remarried. We just celebrated our fourth anniversary. I found a man who loves me and my children unconditionally. He loves us despite our hectic schedules, despite all the medical issues, despite all the craziness. In fact, he loves us because of it all. He loves us how a husband and father should. I had been broken so many years ago and I had never been put back together. I had stitched a few seams and bandaged a few others. My soul was severed, and it so desperately needed to be reassembled. He did this for me. My husband now is the opposite of what I had the first time. There are no games, no lies, no worry about infidelity. Total trust. Let me say that again - total trust. It hasn't always been easy. There isn't a manual or a course you take for getting remarried when you're forty and both have ex-spouses and children, but we figure it out. Both of us came with baggage, and there have been many times that baggage has made itself known. Sometimes it is just a little whisper that is easy to ignore and other times it is a mighty roar that must be faced head-on.

Two years ago, with the encouragement of my husband and kids, I went back to school and got trained as a family mediator. It was one of the scariest experiences of my life, but also one of the most rewarding. After fighting the family court system for seven years, I finally felt like I was on the right side of it. It was an eye-opening experience and one that has given me the education and resources to help many women going through the process of separation and divorce. If I had allowed it, my first husband and our divorce could have swallowed me whole. Had I not found my courage and listened to my inner voice, I don't know where I would be today. I don't hold onto a lot of resentment towards my first husband. I am who I am today because of what I went through with him, and I like who I am. I am no longer afraid to use my voice and stand up for what I believe in. I no longer believe in the destiny of my childhood. I have found the faith I lacked as a child and as a young adult. I am secure in my ability to not repeat the mistakes and misconceptions of my past.

I now love my life.

The Courage to Change

GROWTH AND
TRANSITION

Sherry Corbitt

S herry Corbitt doesn't consider herself your average Mortgage Broker. An entrepreneur for nineteen years, she has dipped her toe in the water of many fields, from realtor to journalist to marketing manager. But her real calling was found eleven years ago when she became a mortgage agent and she hasn't looked back since. She loves getting a great mortgage for her clients, but what's more, she cares deeply about them and treats them as she would a close friend. Always looking for a way to help her clients, she became a Divorce Financial Analyst. Filling a gap in the industry and lending support to people during a very traumatic time in their life. Sherry is a Broker and has 8 Mortgage Agents that are part of her team. An active member of the community, she hosts community yard sales, magically charity galas for children, and is a supporter of the

Durham Humane Society. When she is not drawing outside the lines, she loves to travel with her family who are all Disney obsessed.

Goal Slayer
by Sherry Corbitt

"You can't do that. No one would want to hear you speak."

"This is just a shiny, new toy for you to chase. Focus on the marketing plan already in place."

"What would you even talk about?"

"Great to have a dream, but come on, Sherry, this one's a bit of a stretch even for you."

That is what I expected to hear from my Mastermind group when we were at a business retreat planning how to kill it in 2017. But it wasn't what they said, not even close.

After a busy day of business planning, using S.M.A.R.T goal tracking, poring over calendars to schedule the year to the fullest with blog posts, charity events, networking opportunities and client-based touch points, we were now at my favourite but equally nerve wracking part of our two day business retreat.

The B.H.A.G..

Time to speak up and own your Big Hairy Audacious Goal.

Not sure what a B.H.A.G. is? Think of a goal or dream you have that makes you want to throw up just by imagining it. That's a B.H.A.G..

It tickles at the back of your brain, like an annoying little mosquito in the darkness you can't see and try hard to ignore but can't. Maybe you haven't articulated it yet, even to yourself, but it's there.

We all have aspirations that seem so far out of reach that we can fantasize about them, but feel safe knowing that, deep down, they most likely will never come true. It's easy to daydream but what if that dream could come true? Are you ready for it? If the obstacle was removed, would you step forward and embrace your dream?

I had a dream that played around in my head for a long time until the day I actually put it into words and told others.

Do you live by the belief that everything you want is on the other side of fear? This is my story on embracing a dream, pushing through the fear, and getting to the other side because no one can describe what having pride in an achievement means to them. It is too personal to articulate the feeling, but my deepest hope is that you have a dream and find the courage to go after it.

So on that February retreat in 2017, sitting around a table with my four Mastermind rock stars, the conversation turned and suddenly the big question was "If there were no limits, restrictions or all that negative bull crap that holds us back, what would be your B.H.A.G.?"

With a lot of 'uhms' and 'ahs', I finally managed to string together a sentence: "I think I want to try and speak publicly."

Silence.

As soon as the words left my mouth, a part of me wanted to snatch them right back.

Stupid, stupid, stupid. Why did I want to speak in front of people? What would I possibly say? There was nothing of value I could educate people on, so why put an ounce of energy into my already crammed life on a goal that was just stupid and foolish?

"Wow. You'd be a phenomenal speaker."

"Totally you Sherry! What do you want to speak on?"

"Let's make a list of where you can speak and start researching if any of them need conference speakers coming up".

"That takes guts! You'll kill it."

Wait. What?

It takes a lot to make me speechless, but all I could think was: oh boy, did I just say that and wait, did they just support it?

Let's be honest, not every idea I bring to the table at Mastermind is supported. That is the key aspect to an outstanding Mastermind peer support group. You have to be honest and give real feedback, even when it isn't the popular opinion. I knew I could trust these ladies to tell me the truth, even if it wasn't what I wanted to hear. So, their reaction was shocking to me. They liked it!

Maybe they saw the passion I was trying to hide, but once it was out there and spoken, I knew this goal had power. It was my truth. I felt like I had something to say and share but no clue *what*.

And then my girls, like they always do, got the ball rolling. We spent the next while trying to figure out what my hidden talent or unique insight was that could somehow be turned into a speaking proposal. Who did I want to speak in front of? What would they want to hear from me?

Since I love to learn, my compass was pointing me to speak on something educational. Maybe not to kids, but to fellow business owners. I didn't feel like I had any significant hardships that another entrepreneur wouldn't have had to overcome, so speaking about something inspirational didn't sit well with me.

Okay, we had the target audience: other business owners.

Next step: what could I speak on where they might learn something?

If someone is going to give you their most valuable resource, which is their time, I sure as heck wasn't going to take that responsibility lightly. I wanted to dive deep and find the best knowledge I could share.

We decided to discuss what strengths I had. I'll be honest, this was a bit hard for me but if anyone was going to be honest and give me raw feedback, it was going to be these ladies.

Then, like the lens of a camera coming into focus, it hit me. *Marketing.*

I've joked many times before that my least favourite part of being a Mortgage Broker is doing mortgages. I enjoy matchmaking the product to the client, or finding the perfect solution to a problem, but my true passion that gets me up each morning is the marketing side of the business. How do I get my phone to ring over someone else's? Am I bringing myself to the table and making real connections to the people I work with?

It starts with knowing your ideal client. Knowing who you want to spend your time and energy on.

Mic drop. Okay, ladies, we have a winner!

My first speaking proposal would be "*How to Stand Out in a Saturated Market.*"

I am known for being multi-focused and having some... let's call them unique marketing ideas. As a Mortgage Broker, it can be a bit of a head-scratcher to some peers why I host luxurious charity galas for children, run community-wide yard sales, or have a poop emoji on my business card.

I do it because I am authentic to my own voice. I may not be to everyone's taste and that's okay. I have worked hard to have my own personality in what is traditionally a very competitive, male -dominated industry and a relatively boring business for marketing. Dealing with mortgages is serious. You're handling someone's biggest financial asset and their shelter. I like to market deeper than that and focus on the feeling– the pride, the hope that homeownership brings.

To stand out, you have to know your ideal client (and yourself) and then gear your marketing message to them.

As I wrote the speaking proposal, I was always mindful of whether or not I was saying something new or just rehashing what others before me have already said. I tried to add some "Sherry" spice to it and geared my message to other mortgage professionals. I left nothing off the table. I shared my successes, my mistakes, and my challenges along the way. As they say, experience is the name given to your mistakes, so why not share what I have learned (sometimes the expensive way)?

Once, someone told me that if you want to speak professionally, find a problem someone has and fix it. Well, as Mortgage Brokers, our biggest competition are the banks. They have oodles of money to throw into marketing but what they do not have, in my opinion, is personality. Marketing is simply a competition for people's attention. At the end of the day, it isn't the rate that wins a deal. It's how I've made the client feel.

The proposal was done and I was secretly happy with it, but my nerves and that ugly mistress called doubt kept popping up and whispering in my head. What credentials did I have to speak to others? I don't have a degree in marketing. I'm not already an established and proven speaker. My voice is too squeaky. I'm too chubby. I snort when I laugh and I laugh when I'm nervous so, basically, I would just be a chubby, snorting, squeaky speaker with nothing of value to say on the stage.

Oh. My. God. Why do I even want to do this? Delete. Delete. Delete. Let's pretend this never happened and I can go back to my safe place of daydreaming about it instead.

Could I go back? Sure. But I'd made a misstep. I'd made going back into my safe zone not possible. I'd already told my Mastermind group about it and my failure to even try would make them disappointed in me. I'd be disappointed in myself too. If there is one thing I hate more than anything, it's failing.

Let me be clear on something though. At this point, it wasn't even about getting a speaking opportunity. It was about pressing send and putting it out there. Not getting accepted anywhere wasn't a failure, not trying was.

This is the point that a lot of people turn around, when suddenly the line is in front of you and you aren't sure you can cross it. Most people step back into their comfort zone and pat themselves on the back for having come this far. Give a few high fives, big smiles because they haven't made it here before. Look how much you did this time? Good job! Now it's time to regroup and hit it again soon but for now, you deserve to take a tiny break.

Or...

You keep going.

Failing or succeeding isn't the question, just doing is. No one can make you do it. This is between you and future you because it's the future you that will be disappointed if you don't cross that line right this freaking minute.

That is the point I was at. I had my finished proposal and I could see myself up on stage sharing this information and educating others on how to be unique to their marketing voice. All I had to do now was find a place to submit my proposal and hope they wanted to hear from me.

When I started my search, I went to the top of my dream list: Mortgage Professionals of Canada. Every year, the Mortgage Professionals of Canada hosts a conference where thousands of professionals across Canada attend. Speaking there would be the ultimate achievement.

I was aiming high when I hit that submit button but hey, go big or go home! At least I'd now crossed the line and my future self couldn't say that I'd wussed out.

A few weeks had passed and I submitted to a local business development organization that had put out a call for speakers. I heard back almost immediately that I was accepted! Come early November, I would be speaking at *Do It in Durham* to small business owners in my community. I was so excited and very proud of myself for having put it out there and having been chosen.

Ahh, it felt good to be a B.H.A.G. slayer! I posted on my social media account that I was going to be speaking and wham!... another offer came in. It was for me to be on a panel with other Mortgage Professionals called *Zero to Hero* and share how we went from a few deals a year to being a seasoned agent. It was going to be in October and would be in front of about 400 people. Being part of a panel helped my nervousness and I was so excited for the opportunity.

Then the phone rang again. It'd been about two months since I had submitted my proposal for the Mortgage Professionals of Canada National Conference and I had assumed that my little proposal had been declined among the many they received.

Here's the thing about worrying about failing at your dream, you can't really fail because just doing it is a win. When I thought no news meant "thanks, but no thanks," I wasn't upset because I was still proud of myself for having at least tried.

So when the call came that they'd love for me to present at the national conference in Niagara Falls that November, I nearly threw up! I was at our campground and after politely accepting the offer and hanging up, I went tearing through camp telling anyone I could find what had happened. I am pretty sure most had no idea what I was saying, but I didn't care. This was news worth sharing!

Fast forward to November. I spoke at the *Do It in Durham* event to about twenty-five people. I had geared the presentation to work for any business owner, but was nervous that when I got to the audience participation part that there would be crickets. Luckily, the group was very interactive and it was just like speaking to a group of friends. The audience participated and together we laughed, I stumbled, we shared some ah-ha moments, and at the end, people stayed to chat with me about what they'd learned. If there was a cloud ten, I was on it!

The next week I was off to Niagara Falls to present at the conference. Thankful for having done a presentation the week before, I assumed my nerves would be less, but they were intensified by 100! Now I was speaking to peers, mentors, and the best of the best in our industry from across Canada. I felt like a complete fraud.

I wasn't a mega agent.

I wasn't even a Broker who ran her own team.

I was just a little agent in a small town who did weird marketing.

Kill me now.

There was nothing I could do but go through it and let me tell you, I was absolutely terrified! I had never experienced anything like this before. My nerves were making me jittery and it certainly didn't help when I saw the roster of speakers for the conference. We had industry juggernauts speaking and our keynote speaker was the former Prime Minister of Canada, Stephen Harper.

Anxiety? Check.

I got to the conference and was handed my name tag. Attached under my name tag was a silky, beautiful ribbon that said 'Speaker'. It was that exact moment everything changed. I was now a professional speaker. The nerves did not disappear, but pride bubbled up and helped lessen it. This was real. I couldn't deny that only eight months ago I'd had spoken about a vision. I'd worked hard to make it happen, and now it was here.

I deserved my golden ribbon and I wore it with pride. Since I wasn't speaking until the third day of the conference, I was asked many times what my speech was about and the nods and smiles of approval helped me through the anxiety.

I had the stage for forty-five minutes and it flew by. The moderator gave me a two-minute warning at the end and I clicked through the last few slides, recapping what I'd been discussing and wrapped up. People applauded and when we announced that there was no time left for questions, people stayed behind to come up and ask. I stayed in the room for over a half hour chatting, shaking hands, and hearing other people share some of their very cool marketing ideas.

It didn't matter that I wasn't a professional speaker who was polished and articulate with well-timed jokes and an inspiring life-changing message. They saw my passion and loved it. It felt amazing!

I returned from the conference ready to finish the year strong and start the new year with even more energy. At that time, speaking wasn't really part of my plan moving forward. I felt like I'd climbed a mountain, reached the peak, enjoyed the view, and was ready to go back to the real world.

Part of me wanted to speak again, part of me was worried that I could never top a national conference so why try?

I could have stopped there and been truly happy. I really could have. The B.H.A.G. had been slayed and I was ready for a shiny, new thing to chase.

Then a call came in January that I could never have imagined. Mortgage Professionals of Canada was planning their symposiums and wanted to know if I was available to come and speak for them. They wanted to pay for me to come with them to Nova Scotia, Toronto, Saskatoon, Winnipeg, Alberta, and Vancouver.

Shut the front door!

Turns out that after the national conference, the surveys received said I was a very well-liked speaker and they wanted to bring me with them on a cross-country tour. People loved the topic I spoke on and wanted to hear more! Less than a year from that Mastermind planning session where I said I wanted to try speaking in public, I would be a national speaker. Was this really happening? How could I say no?!

Here's the thing. I had way more reasons to say no than I did to say yes. I have a young family at home. I have a business to run. Employees to manage. Clients to care for.

But I had one huge reason to say yes. Deny it or not, I wanted to do it. I loved speaking on stage. It's hard for most of us to admit when we're good at something. Our modesty stops us from giving ourselves a pat on the back. I enjoyed speaking and this was going to be a once in a lifetime offer so, if I could make it work with my job and family, then I just had to do it.

Best experience of my life! In 2018, I was on 16 flights for work jetting across this beautiful country. I met the most amazing people in my industry, gained a confidence in my own work and business I never had before, and learned so much from the other speakers.

In Banff, my mom and a girlfriend came with me and we turned it into a mini girl's trip. We stayed right at the Fairmont Chateau Lake Louise, the most stunning hotel and place I'd ever been in my life. One of my absolute favourite memories for the rest of my life will be of my mom having a hysterical freak-out going up the side of a mountain on a gondola. As a seasoned traveller, my breath was taken away at the natural beauty that Canada had to offer. In Vancouver, I dined at a restaurant over the ocean and in Nova Scotia, I dipped my toes in the sea at Peggy's Cove. In Alberta, I stood on the very peak of a mountain feeling on top of the world.

When I first spoke about my goal to be a professional speaker, never in my wildest imagination could I have foreseen where it would take me. Maybe in the future I will explore speaking more. Maybe my next goal will be to become recognized as an international speaker and get paid to speak somewhere with a beach!

You wouldn't have picked up this book if you weren't looking for a change. Think of a goal, a dream, something that is so far from reality you can't even fully picture it in your mind yet. Now add some details to it. Put a name to it.

What would make this dream not possible? List the reasons that could stop you, then tackle each item on that list one at a time.

Can't afford it? Start saving. Take credit and borrow. Barter.

Don't have time? Delegate. Get up earlier. Hire a babysitter for 3 hours a week to focus. Get a house cleaner and free up a few hours. Stay up later.

Don't have support in your life? I honestly believe this is the easiest one to overcome because you don't know you don't have the support until you tell someone your dream. Give them a chance to prove you wrong.

Don't have the courage? Read this book and hear the stories of these women, just like you, who found the courage to speak their truth, own their decisions, and made their dreams happen.

Now for the toughest questions you must honestly answer. Take a few minutes to really give these questions the attention they deserve.

1 - If this dream doesn't come true, what would happen in your life? If you don't pursue it, would anything change? How does that make you feel? Are you ready to subscribe to the belief that it is better to live a life of 'at least I tried' instead of 'I wish I had'?

2 - What would happen if you did pursue this dream and it didn't work out? Would it bankrupt you? Be harmful to your health? Crush your soul? Kill you? It will probably not completely destroy your world if it doesn't work out. So why not try it?

3 - What would happen if you did pursue this dream and it did work out? Your dream will have been achieved! You'll have made it happen! Anything is possible. Just remember that all your dreams are on the other side of fear.

Do nothing and have exactly what you have now. Do something and if it doesn't work out, you'll feel accomplished for having tried. Do something and if it happens, you get to be B.H.A.G. slayer.

Write it down. Believe it. Work hard toward your vision. Make it happen.

I believe in you.

Shandel Shand

Shandel Shand is a two-time business owner, the first company she created specializes in Airbnb Cleaning Her entrepreneurship journey and life experience motivated her to start mentoring 19-29 year olds who are feeling stuck in their personal and professional success. Shandel's coaching and consulting business, 'InspiredbyShandel' gives mentees resources, skills and an aggressive action plan to achieve what they desire in their twenties. She is also a public speaker who offers insight on subjects related to growing through adversities, giving yourself permission to start dominating life and how to get really great at getting what you desire. In addition, her passion includes advocacy for social justice and respecting women in business in which she contributes her free time to spreading awareness, providing expertise on social media platforms and leading by example.

The Better Side of Me
by Shandel Shand

*"I am no longer accepting the things I cannot **change**.*
*I am **changing** the things I cannot accept."*
— Angela Davis

How I fulfill my purpose is through my commitment to act on what I truly desire. Purpose is a word a lot of people are intimidated by. Of course, it's intimidating! I agree, especially when recognizing we all have a lot to offer! We all have more than one specific talent. I know I'm not alone with this.

I used to wonder why was I the doomed one compared to others. Titles always seemed odd to me. Society seems to want to have us define ourselves by our profession. This may be what confused me most about understanding my value.

Doctors, lawyers, the self-employed, and street hustlers all had one thing in common in my eyes. They were human, and they made mistakes. Some lived full and free lives, while others have ended up in jail, struggled with mental health, lost their families trust, recycled toxic bad habits, relationships and friendships. We all transition when our time here is up. It can't be our profession that defines us. Rather the decisions we make to become who we are today and what we are proud to leave behind as our legacy- this is what we should aim to be remembered for.

My name is Shandel Shand. I'd like to introduce myself not so you know my name, but you recognize that's who I am. There is only one me, and there is only one you. I am unique and trying to navigate life as any other person is. Life is hard but I believe we are our most powerful in the depths of despair.

The steps that I took during my willingness to change initially began in desperation. I was inspired to shift and had accepted getting uncomfortable to truly transform. I became persistent to do things I'd never done before such as counselling, building a business, volunteering and public speaking. Each step uncovered vulnerable layers of me and parts of my story I was willing to share with the world.

My final step was to surround myself with people who had what I wanted and to continue to be grateful for everyone and everything that shaped who I am and will continue to become. We relate to many of those that have a common past, but I've heard it said that it's best to seek those with a common future moving forward.

It took me three long years to regain my dignity and win a criminal court case. I had been in trouble with the law between ages 21-24. I lived with PTSD, depression, anxiety and the possible reality of facing jail time. Everyday, I was confused and having flashbacks questioning how my life had sunk so deep. In my mind, I was looking for someone or something to blame. Maybe it was a few life experiences in childhood that threw off my better judgement. Or perhaps it was "friends," as I freshly turned 18, who glamorized the fast-cash life. Even though my thoughts searched for answers, the devastation remained: "Why me!?". The fact was, I was the only person who could take responsibility and control of my life to grow from where I was. There are no excuses or blame that give you the juicy rewards accountability and dedication to personal growth give you.

For the first year adapting to attending court frequently and waiting on my trial was unmanageable. After being arrested I was released on bail for almost 3 years and living with restrictions. I was in my early twenties and had an 11pm curfew. I lived in fear of the authorities controlling my life. At times, improving my life felt pointless. Some of the ugliest parts of my life were out of the dark and I needed to make life beautiful again in all aspects. I had nothing more to lose but everything to gain while proceeding with my legal situation. I was rock bottom low.

During most judicial proceedings, the accused criminal is offered a plea deal. This offer is much better than what happens to you if you lose at your trial. Can you imagine had I lost at my trial? I would not be writing this chapter, and still serving my sentence. I was extremely uncomfortable the day I turned my plea deal down, not because of my innocence but because of my vision about days like today. Turning it down meant a longer sentence if I was going to lose. I was feeling as if I was throwing away the good moments in my life that hadn't happened yet!

I almost plead guilty to get the whole mess over with! I'm grateful that, at the last second, I literally found it too difficult to accept. Life would continue to pass and people would move forward, everyone but me. I would be in a completely different cold world, unable to share my gifts, to accomplish my goals, or to serve any benefit to the community at all. Being in trouble with the law or in jail is like being in a different world.

In childhood we heard, what doesn't kill you makes you stronger. They were right about that but only if you believe it to be true. We can predict a life of misery for those who don't unlock their strength.

When I was a kid, most of the household bills were paid on time and my parents worked hard to make sure our fridge was always full. I always had somewhere to live despite a frequent dysfunctional environment. I'm not ready to give detail about my childhood/teenage years due to my PTSD. This is something I am still coping with.

I thought I lived an average life and believed every family had major issues behind closed doors. There was a lot of concealing of how challenging things were at home. As I got older, I took advantage of being able to stay out late or sleep out. I figured it would be less headache for myself and the household to be out of the way and try and make it on my own.

In university, the need for money to have more freedom became certain to me. I think back and realize how clouded my head must've finally become after years of trying to convince myself I've lived a "normal" or "average" life. My family and I are far from normal but still very loving even after dark times. I've learnt how to live with setting my boundaries and barriers with my family to ensure the most helpful communication.

Life can never be perfect. Throughout life, there were times I'd faced significant disadvantages for a young woman to be successful. Although recognizing these hurdles, the court continued to pursue a trial. In spite of my unstable life, the court had no sympathy.

Challenging situations and my own thoughts about them nearly killed me, whether it be stress or suicidal thoughts. It was through my legal situation that I started believing much sooner than most that the set of cards I was holding was not my final deal. Life had not been absolutely terrible, but if the hard times were worth living this far, I felt power in knowing what enjoying life could actually be like.

A large part of my life change has to do with believing in myself while noticing others believed in me to be better and do better now, no matter the life circumstances. The cards we are dealt will always change and have the potential to give us a winning hand. Life is a gamble and I've learnt from my losses now prepared to share how to be resilient and *grow through what you go through*. I created a sturdy foundation of decisions I believed would result in a more enjoyable and fruitful life.

My perspective on life was impacted by mentorship. My doomed mindset shifted to noticing my confidence and this became contagious to those around me. Although life was running me over and reversing, determination did not let my adversities define me. My mentors, and the professionals around me admired my confidence. The women in my trauma counselling group sessions admired my self-awareness and resilience.

I was reminded I was worthy and deserving of feeling loved for being me. I desired to add more value to the lives of others when noticing the strong impact my positive decisions had in my life. I recognized how it contributed to the people around me. The results were enough to continue this new, exciting and rewarding route in life and be mindful of my legacy. I became focused and clear on the paths I believed would help me. People were willing to help guide me when I was lost and felt the world was against me.

And I did feel lost. In fact, I felt hopeless. The only empty words people would often offer me were, "have hope".

Health and freedom are two things I'm most grateful for. My thoughts were not always so resilient and positive. I felt as if I'd have an easier time escaping to the moon than to find hope or strength. I resisted personal development and my mental health was suffering. When the law was in conflict with me, I was not looking forward to life.

How to overcome this disastrous nightmare? At the time, I couldn't tell you. With legal trouble came a lawyer. Something he said stuck with me: "Act as if nothing is happening. That's all you can do." He knew little about me but could see in me what I wanted most: to get back in the driver seat, change my life, and go forward regardless of knowing that, in reality, the legal matter was out of my hands and ongoing.

Another philosophical and respected quote in my lifetime, "Get your sh*t! together," said another lawyer, Ms. Thomas. They made me feel like family giving me both gentle and tough love. Ms. Thomas didn't like when I called her "mom" jokingly, and if this were to be a Hollywood movie, she would choose Rihanna to play her role. I know because we spoke about it during one of our many trial prep meetings month after month. She was my lawyer but served more than justice.

We communicated a lot and spent a lot of time together. These meetings most people would find it difficult to muster a smile. I found it more difficult to be sad all the time. I would tell her my "criminal" case would be a pretty good movie- if all the drama was not happening to me, that is. She thought I was nuts so many times, but her judgements of me or my case never prevented her from helping me. In fact, she had supplied me with a list of resources to seek professional assistance to help me heal.

I was in contact with an organization that provided me with counselling. There I was able to talk my experiences through, blame myself less, and actually begin my entrepreneurship journey of goal-setting and building a business. I discovered healing would be a lifelong process. Finding healing is not just one step but an ongoing endeavour.

The most impactful moment in my life was one day at court witnessing someone else accept their plea deal. Although sorted with counselling sessions, support, and progress, that day brought me back to reality. I was feeling defeated. I had been going through life and its motions as if nothing was happening. I was rebuilding a foundation for myself to have hope but even then, on an upward journey, life felt impossible.

Despite a difficult day ahead, the weather was beautiful. Spring was around the corner and I was in one of my favourite neighbourhoods in the city. I had planned a lunch at my favourite restaurant knowing my morning was going to be rough. No matter how strong we believe we are, some days just are not easy.

I left court with intentions to proceed with my regular schedule. I tried and gave up quickly as the sun was still shining. I had a moment of desperation, feeling stuck, replaying experiences that have not gone so well in life. Then, imagining how it would feel to be convicted, jailed, put away and watch them throw away the key, I drifted. I found it to be a numbing feeling.

I was completely unaware of the greatness and beauty of abundance around me. All I could feel was stuck. I was set on the idea I deserved to call it quits and wanted to walk in front of traffic. I'd save everyone and myself the time and energy worrying about me. There are no other options, I thought. I've been wrong about a lot of things in life. Just as I was wrong in thinking my only solution was suicide. I decided not to walk in front of traffic even though I felt so deeply it was the right answer; I stayed standing on the sidewalk stuck. I made a phone call to a crisis hotline number Ms. Thomas had given me.

Cars and people kept moving fast through rush hour, and I stood still, cemented to the ground. But I had made the decision, to call an organization trained to assist women in crisis. Crisis was an understatement. However, the woman on the phone was trained and ready for a wreck like me. She, too, possibly saved my life. Her only concern was my safety, not asking anything of me, except for me not to hang up the phone.

Most organizations have long wait-lists to see a counsellor. The odds somehow working in my favor, they had an appointment cancel which opened conveniently for me to show up. There was something in me that wanted to live much more than I wanted to die. The tone of the day had changed with a few interactions from strangers willing to listen. I met women in situations similar to mine and I realized I was not alone. I was not the one doomed. People in fact were going through much worse than me. I couldn't feel bad for myself.

It became my mission to want to encourage other women to persevere through their hardships. It became my mission to share how entrepreneurship and mentorship possibly saved my life. I appreciated having lawyers, counsellors and peers see something in me that I had forgotten in myself.

I had found a tribe at the organization that saved my life. Counsellors noticed my skills and experiences and used me to help build what is one of my favorite accomplishments. I was asked to volunteer and help train women who were committed to operate a "Talk and Listen" crisis hotline. This helped incarcerated women gain access toll-free, and women in the community needing assistance.

I was so involved with volunteering, that I was easily distracted from my trial. The day I was free to go, one of the first phone calls I received was from the organization. They offered me a part-time job to help facilitate a workshop for women to have a safe space to drop in weekly. Something they did not know before offering me the job was the day I received their contact info, I was going to attend the same drop-in as a client. A year and a half later, I was given the opportunity to run the drop-in and get paid.

Within the time I would have been jailed, I've been featured on CBC radio and various podcasts advocating for prison reform. I spoke for the United Way at their launch of United Women Toronto and York Region, and Master Degree Classes at Universities. I've had plenty of opportunities to speak to audiences about subjects I'm passionate about, such as entrepreneurship, mental health and crisis.

I became known for hosting and attending many events in the community surrounding, mental health, prison reform, and helping women with project life. I opened my first business and grew to open a second business catered to help coach others get unstuck in life and business.

I am most proud of being a big help in launching a Crisis Hotline for women to access resources or simply have someone to speak to. These are a few highlights of a large list of accomplishments I would need another chapter for.

Not everyone will unlock their courage to make changes. I can imagine a lot of us wait for inspiration or desperation to change as I did. I encourage change much faster. There are key moments in life where you'll unlock your courage when necessary. A power we doubted we have.

I am most grateful for the day I was free to go that I received a job offer from an organization that was there for me in crisis. Not only did I operate my business, I had a part-time income and something positive to occupy my time. I felt like there was no turning back. I had excelled while volunteering and success has been a domino effect ever since. I think of it as life rewarding me for not giving up.

I truly believe there are many moments in life where we will continue to face pain, fear, and uncertainty. But through community, confidence and the courage to change, we can gain strength. Having hope in life is hard. Feeling hopeless is difficult too. We can decide which hard life we want to live everyday.

> *"You will face many defeats in life,*
> *but never let yourself be defeated."*
> *— Maya Angelou*

Erin Rodgers (Rochon)

Erin Rodgers(Rochon) is a mother, business owner and wife. In her spare time she enjoys camping, hiking, random road trips and spending time with friends and family. With many ups and downs in the rollercoaster of life, she always keeps positive and tries to see the good in every situation. Everything that crosses our path is a learning experience and although we don't always see it as such at the time, when we reflect back we can most often feel happy to have made it through and learned the lesson that presented itself. Erin lives a life with no regrets, and is often credited for the strength she has had in overcoming so many obstacles that have been thrown her way, yet she never gave up.

Erin operates a Boutique Bookkeeping firm in Toronto, Ontario called Rochon & Associates. Servicing small to medium size business owners with their bookkeeping, staffing, and process management. She loves helping business owners build and scale their business and get them back to their "why"! No matter what stage of business you are in Rochon & Associates can assist you to get to the next stage.

Erin hopes you enjoy this chapter and find the strength and courage to listen to your intuition, and try and see the bigger picture no matter what obstacle is put in your way.

Listen, Reflect and Learn
by Erin Rodgers (Rochon)

As humans, it is our nature to often become complacent and just let the life we have established control our daily routines no matter how mundane, unexcited or unhappy we are doing so. We tend to look at the traditional version of what we are *supposed* to do and are afraid to make any of those changes for fear of the unknown and public perception.

For years this was me. At 20, I found myself looking at where I was supposed to go next with my life. I had been dating someone since the age of 17, and we loved each other as best we knew at that age. So, of course, our next step was marriage. It was the expected thing of us from our family and our network. We were regular churchgoers, so moving in together before marriage was an absolute faux pas. If we wanted to move to that step, we had to get married. Next thing I knew it was the day of the wedding and, in my gut, I knew that this wasn't where I wanted to be. But instead of following that gut feeling, I dismissed it as wedding jitters and looked at the sea of people in the church and told myself there was no way I could not follow through. I would be disappointing so many. Not to mention all the money we spent and how that would all be for naught. So, down the aisle I went, and I committed myself to a lifetime marriage with someone I knew deep down I wasn't completely happy with.

Well, as I am sure you can guess, the marriage didn't last. We quickly grew apart and started to want different things in our lives. We became roommates over partners and in a way, started to resent each other. We maintained the marriage because we had to. We kept it going because it was a lifetime commitment and to us, divorce would never be an option. I knew I had to continue to try and make it work, and try to be the best wife that I could be to hopefully turn things around.

After five years of marriage, things came to an abrupt stop. The week before Christmas, my husband came to me with tears in his eyes to tell me that he couldn't do it any longer. Although it wasn't something we often talked about, we both knew, that neither of us was happy anymore. Earlier in the marriage, we talked about wanting children and a family which was really important to me, but he no longer wanted this. He didn't want to hurt me, but he couldn't keep living the life that we were living. My husband wanted to change, and he found the courage to make that change. A change that I had avoided and denied for so long. I was crushed. I told myself I was doing enough to keep the marriage whole, but I knew deep down I was living a lie. To our network of friends and family, this news also came as a complete shock. You see, we were living two different lives. From the outside perspective, we were the dream couple-always doing things together. We seemed so happy and we seemed so in love. But that was only a façade for those in the outside world. When we were alone, and at home, this was not us. We were rarely in the same room, never doing anything together except maybe eating dinner together the odd night.

It took me time to overcome this new reality. It hurt my soul that he had the courage to break this marital covenant and had the ability to choose his happiness. He seemed so selfish to me at the time, but I know now, that he was strong and he was right.

Fast forward to a few years later when I found myself in almost the same predicament, but this time with a newborn. We were married, we were not happy, and we were not living life together. He barely had any real interactions with our newborn and boy did he resent me. He felt as though there was suddenly so much pressure on him, and he was not happy that I had to focus so much time on our baby. He felt neglected but didn't make any attempts to fix things. I knew this wasn't a happy marriage or one that dreams were made of, but again I had that fear of making a change- especially now that there was a child involved. So, because I had that fear, and I refused to make the change myself, the universe made the shift for me. One morning, when my son was just nine months old, I woke up to an email saying he was leaving and would be back that afternoon to pick up his things. *What?* Are you kidding me? How in the hell can someone seriously wake up and make a decision like that? I couldn't even fathom it. But again, deep down I knew it was right. He was a coward in the way he handled this. He didn't have the strength to talk to me in person, but knew he had to make this decision for his well-being. It was more than selfish; not thinking about the impact to me, but more importantly, to his son. In the end, though, it was the best decision. He has remained selfish in his living and is not involved in my son's life at all, which has its impact, but overall we are much better off the way this ended.

After this last marriage breakdown, I vowed that I wouldn't do the whole marriage thing again and that I was going to be a lot more selective with the relationships that I entered. This time would be different. I had more confidence, and I knew that it was ok for me to choose *me* and that it was acceptable to have personal expectations about my partner and our relationship. I did a lot of soul-searching and figuring out what was going on in my life at this point. I discovered that I needed to find the courage inside to be able to make these sometimes terrifying choices for myself and not wait for the other person to do it. I had a yearning to be that brave- to be able to step out of my comfort zone and take a risk towards the unknown. I had survived two divorces now and knew in my heart of hearts that if I could overcome this, then I could initiate the changes needed to live a happy, joyful life. We always hear people saying that anything is possible and the world only gives us things that we can handle. How often do we balk at that concept when we are going through these hurdles in life? Then when we are finally out on the other side, we realize just how much better we are and think, if only I saw the light sooner!

About a year after my second marriage ended, I found myself in another committed relationship. It was during this relationship that I finally hit my breaking point. This relationship was my Ah-ha moment, and I finally saw the light. This time, there was a lot more at risk, though. Not only did we have my son, but we also had joint custody of his two children. My son was super close to his step-siblings, and of course, we were a very well-blended and close-knit family. Things started going downhill about two years into the relationship when I realized that I wasn't happy. I was not feeling fulfilled and there was just something missing. So, rather than sit back, try harder on my part thinking I was the only problem, I spoke up. I reached outside of my comfort level, deep within my soul, and rather than placing all the blame on myself as I previously did, I spoke my truth. I sat down with him and let him know that I was unhappy. I needed basic things from him that he wasn't providing me. I told him that if we weren't able to make the changes and work on these things, then I would have to think about leaving the relationship. This was really hard for me. It was not only going to impact me, but also three children who had already been through so much loss and change in their early years. It felt wrong for me to be so selfish- to only think about myself and my feelings, but I knew I should be valued in this relationship, and I knew I deserved more. So I asked for it. My partner at the time was actually very receptive to my concerns, and the last thing he wanted was to end the relationship. He saw what I was saying, and he promised to make a valiant effort at helping me through the tough time, and he would work on being a better partner for us and for our family. This worked for a while, and he truly did step up. But it couldn't last as it wasn't truly who he was. Then we started going through some changes in our professional lives which shook the boat even more.

217

You see, I was not only unhappy in my relationship, but I was also unhappy in my career. I was working outside of my area and having to commute sometimes up to two hours to and from work. I was having to miss time with my son and seeing him grow up, and for the first two and a half years of his life, for the most part, someone else was raising him. This hurt my heart, and I knew I needed to make a change. So I thought long and hard about what to do. I looked for work locally, but the financial hit our family would take wasn't possible, so I had to look at other options. I then found myself laid off of work, and completely lost. My partner and I had many conversations about what I could potentially do, and while I was trying to figure that out, I started thinking about the skills I had learned from my previous work experience. I went to the job boards and started looking for part-time freelance work so that I could have a bit more control over my hours, and not be doing the same thing for the same people every day. See, I am the type of person who likes variety, who likes new surroundings and who likes to have a bit more control over my life. I found that I really wasn't a great *employee.*

Eventually, I found an admin job working for a contracting company three and a half days a week. This was a great start. I went in, worked for four hours doing things I was good at, and of course, taking on additional tasks as the weeks went on and getting paid what I was worth. I then started thinking about how I could manage another client and what type of tasks I could do. I went back to the job boards and started applying for admin and bookkeeping jobs, and very quickly obtained a second client but this time in bookkeeping. It was in a brand-new industry and had a completely new program that I would have to learn, but I was confident that I could do it. So, I took that job and now had two clients. This quickly morphed into more and next thing I knew I was launching my own business. I never in a million years would have pictured myself being an entrepreneur or a business owner. It wasn't ever even a glimmer in my life's path. But I needed to make that change in my life. I needed to have more flexibility over the hours I worked and the work I did so that I could be the best mom and best wife that I wanted to be.

At first, my partner was supportive of this change and this new direction. But then, as things continued to progress for me and my client base grew, it meant that my income began to grow. And within two years it surpassed his. This didn't go over well. He felt inferior. He was working long hours, commuting to and from work, and wasn't fulfilled in his job. And here I was, working less hours, loving the work I was doing and making more money than him. This started to impact our relationship again and this time it wasn't repairable. We had drifted so far apart and the desire to come back together wasn't really there.

It was not at all an easy decision to make. The kids took the news really hard and that hurt. It made me question my decision and almost made me go back and try again, but I had to stick with my gut and choose my happiness and in the end, the happiness of my son. I wasn't being the mom that I knew I could be. I wasn't happy with my relationship and the life I was living which had a huge impact on the level of patience and involvement that I had with my children. I wasn't interested in being engaged with my partner, friends or any of the children, so I was feeling a significant disconnect with all the personal relationships I had. It was time for another change-another adjustment and another unknown. But this time I was ready. I was in control, and I knew I could overcome any of the obstacles that would come my way.

Once I left the relationship, it felt like a new life was beginning. My business hit an all-time high and was growing so much. I was in a totally different head-space and was ready to take on anything. I was open to whatever life was going to throw my way and was ready to receive abundance. I did a lot of personal work and growth for the next two years.

There was a lot of self-discovery and real work done on how the universe works with us and for us, and that we do have the power to manifest great things in our lives. I consulted with a couple different self-development gurus in my area, and did personal work such as QCP, Time Line Therapy, BEAM Treatments, as well as clearing of some negative thoughts. I also attended a Tony Robbins *Unleash The Power Within Event*, and this was the icing on the cake. I overcame some huge limiting beliefs that were holding me back from living my most amazing life. After all of this, I was ready to start to explore dating again. I saw different men here and there, but didn't want a full relationship. I wanted to get everything else in my life to a point where I was completely happy and on a path of pure joy. Once I had that figured out, I knew it would be time to figure out the relationship piece.

The next transition that presented itself was yet another complete shock and something that threw me for a complete loop. The universe was about to test me about how much I truly had learned over the last couple of years, and if I was able to wholeheartedly get out of my comfort zone and let things happen for me instead of against me. I was at home one Friday afternoon, and had just finished up a project when a phone call came in. I don't often answer when I don't recognize the phone number, but for some reason, I answered this one. The next two hours were the strangest, most uncertain times I think I had ever experienced.

The person on the other line was a complete cold call from a new local business who was interested in purchasing my client list. When I first heard the words, my initial reaction was to laugh, and say, "Fuck, no." I could not even imagine the idea of selling my business. That was my baby. I had worked so hard for the last four years building it and nurturing relationships with my clients. Not to mention, what on earth would I do with my career and life if I sold my business? I had no intention at all at any point of doing something like this. My succession plan was for my son or another child to take over the business when I wanted to retire. The person on the other line was quite surprised at my reaction and really didn't know how to respond. I stated that I would be open to speak with them about collaboration options and how we could potentially work together, but that selling them my full business wasn't something I was interested in. So, she said she would discuss with her business partner and call me back.

I got off that call and just sat in the quiet for a moment. I questioned the universe to say what did this mean? What did this present? Why would this even be an option for me?

I reached out to my closest business friends and asked them what they thought of it, attempting to do some gut checks. Then I came to the realization that I should at least hear them out. I should hear what they were offering and what the stipulations would be before I flat out say no. But, I also said, I would only do that if they called me back. Well, in less than two hours they called back to say they would like to meet with me the following week on Monday to talk about the options. The universe had spoken, and I decided that I was going to be open to discussing the collaboration. At this time I still wasn't quite in a place to say that I was open to hearing about a full sale. I needed to spend the weekend sitting on this and figuring out what I would need to even consider it.

This was scary. It was so out of my comfort zone and took some serious courage to even consider. I was conflicted, unsure, excited, nervous, and I was in shock. I was also a single mom. My son was seven years old and here I was contemplating selling the lifeline to our finances. I was looking at potentially starting over in a completely new field depending on what the offer was or becoming an employee again. I didn't have any idea what they would offer or how it would work, but I needed to be open and receptive to all options.

I spent the weekend thinking and writing and discussing. I called close friends, my parents, and a couple other people in my network who I knew could offer unbiased opinions. One of my close confidants reiterated to me what I deep down knew: *Go in with a plan.* Go in with a minimum and go in with what my stipulations would be and see how open they are to meeting my conditions.

One of the biggest conditions I had was that I wouldn't be forced into an open-ended non-compete which would force me to change industries and career paths completely. I wasn't willing to do that as I really had no idea where I would even go. The other thing I wanted to make sure was that they would keep my staff and keep them on the files they were working on. I didn't want to see five people out of work because of my one decision. And I wanted the clients to be confident in the sale knowing that the same bookkeeper, who was already familiar with their files, would be continuing to work on it, resulting in very little change for them.

I also went in with a dollar figure in mind. I knew where my absolute minimum would be for what I would accept for the purchase price. This was something I wouldn't voice, as of course if they were thinking higher, I didn't want to let them think I would take lower. So I had the number in my mind.

On Monday morning, I got ready. I made sure I was in a comfortable outfit that I felt confident in. I reiterated to myself what my stipulations and conditions were and where I was and wasn't willing to negotiate. I sat down in the boardroom, three of them sitting across from me. My heart racing and still so unsure of how this was going to go, I was nervous. But I was also feeling optimistic. I realized over the weekend that this offer was a huge dream for most business owners, and here I was with an unsolicited, cold-called opportunity after only four years in business. I am not a cocky person, nor am I one to stroke my ego, but I was fucking awesome! I had built a business that caught the attention of someone who wanted to purchase this success. Holy shit! So I was able to walk in, head held high, knowing that I had a great value for them. No low-ball offers would be accepted.

I started the meeting by letting them know that I had done some thinking over the weekend and decided that I was open to discussing and hearing their offer for the sale of the business. This was when things got really interesting. They offered to buy the full client list and keep me on as an employee in a management role, which I, of course, said was not something I was interested in. I knew from previous experience that I am not a great employee, and all I could picture was them wanting to change the processes and the ways in which I handled the clients and our work. This would not be an easy thing for me. So, I declined that and asked what the other options would be.

I let them know that one of the proposals I had was to sell them about 90% of my client list, allowing me to keep 10% of whom were all in very specific industries. This would enable me to continue practicing, and not have to find a new career. To my surprise, they were open to this option and said that they really didn't see any issue with it at all.

Next came the staff. They were at first hesitant to commit to keeping all five staff members. They started with stating that they would have to evaluate it once they had the client list and saw who was working on what, and what

224

hours each was working. I was ok with that and we moved onto the next topic, which was the last make or break money.

To my surprise, they offered to purchase the client list for 100% of its billable value for the last twelve months. Based on the numbers I ran on the weekend, this well surpassed my minimum amount. The only stipulations were that it was 50% payable upfront and 50% payable in one year's time, once they confirmed retention of the clients. There is quite a big amount of risk with this stipulation, so I let them know that things sounded pretty decent to me, and that I would take all the info they had given to me and get back to them in a few days. I really needed to mull it over and get some legal advice to ensure that things would not work against me with the second payout.

I spoke to a business lawyer and to another industry expert, and they both stated to me that the offer was more than fair and that, with the proper, contract things could be pretty cut and dry, and worded in ways that would ensure a fair deal.

So the next couple of weeks were very nerve-racking for me. I was afraid of making the wrong decision- fearful of how the clients would react and worried that they may just jump ship the minute they heard of the sale. I think I was more afraid of what everyone else's reaction and perceptions were than what I was personally feeling.

This was a huge thing for me. This was my baby. I had built it and my reputation with a lot of time, money and effort for the last four years and here I was contemplating throwing it all away and starting fresh. But at the same time, this was such a huge opportunity for me, both financially and personally. It would mean a clean slate for my business, and my son and I. It meant a lot of my time would be freed up, and I wouldn't have the same amount of stress trying to manage close to ninety clients essentially on my own. It meant that I could re-build and correct all the errors I made the first time around, and hopefully make it a much smoother and easier company to operate.

So, after a few more meetings, a lot more soul-searching and discussions with peers, I made the decision that it was a great option and that it was a choice I was going to take. The universe presented me with this option, and as scary and nerve-racking as it was, it was also exciting and encouraging. The running joke with my peer group was that I would just re-build and do it all over again in five years. I guess time will tell.

After the sale of the business, there were bumps in the road and it wasn't the easiest transition, but almost all of my clients took the news well and were ok with the change knowing that their same bookkeeper would remain on their file. They have all completed the transition and are doing well with the new company.

I am happy that I made the decision and proud that I am able to completely focus on the new industries and re-building. It took a lot of courage and a lot of letting go of control to make this decision. I realized though that again, the universe will present us with options and different scenarios and before we flat out say no, or reject the ideas, we should be open to investigating the options and let things come together in the way they are meant to.

A new relationship also came to fruition during the sale of the business. I had been dating as mentioned, but I was far from looking for something serious. I was enjoying the single life, and enjoying being able to meet new people and loved being desired. I had people wanting me to commit, and wanting me to enter into a full relationship, but there was something holding me back. I didn't feel connected enough to make that step with any of them. I had resigned myself to the thought that for the remainder of the year I would remain single, and that in the new year, I would refocus my attention on an actual committed relationship. I made New Years plans with girlfriends and we all said it would be a great girls night out, no boys, and we would just enjoy a fun time together. Well, this is when love finds you; when you least expect it and well, when you don't really want it.

I resisted my now husband for close to two months. Kept him at arm's length just like any other. Kept him close enough but not within my personal bubble. I refused to get vulnerable and refused to accept that this could be anything more than a fling. But this man was persistent. He saw something in me that he couldn't let go of and when we first met, he knew he wanted to marry me. He continued to pursue me no matter how much I pushed back, and even though he knew I wasn't ready. He gave me the space I needed, but he also made sure that I knew he wasn't going anywhere, and that he would be sticking by me until I was ready. It took a couple months, and many many intimate and serious conversations. He helped me discover so many things about myself and who I had become. He was my rock when I didn't know I needed one, and he continues to be the smile that makes my world go round. I had finally found my soulmate. I had envisioned it. I had written it down. I had created a list of my wants, needs and desires and this man fulfilled every single item on those lists.

Once I re-read the list and compared it to him, I knew I had to accept that this was the man I had been longing for. This was my soul mate, and the answer to all my dreams and desires. He treats me like a Queen and values me in ways I never knew were possible.

With all that I have encountered and shared, I encourage everyone to evaluate where you are in life and make a list of the things you aren't happy about. Then, when looking at that list, determine if the items are things you can control, or things that you can't. If they are items that you can control, what would it take to make things better? What would you need to do or say or change to improve that area of your life, your business, your relationship?

Then take the time to think about what your life would look like, feel like, and be like if those things changed.

Picture it. Feel it. Write it down. Then take action. Don't wait.

We all deserve to live our most outstanding life. Get out of the rut of just letting life happen to you. Don't become complacent like so many others do. Make something of yourself and create the most amazing life that you can imagine. Have the courage to change and the fortitude to stick with those changes. You deserve nothing but the best.

Acknowledgements

This book would not have been made possible without the amazing women that answered the call to share their story. The process was not easy for them and I know old wounds were opened, and each and everyone worked through them. I want to say a big thank you for sharing your hearts and stories so the readers are able to learn from them.

I also want to thank our amazing book coach Danielle Scruton that worked with the ladies on their chapters. Guiding them and providing additional writing support through this process, helping them turn their stories into their chapter. She also helped edit their stories to make it ready for our future reader. I am thankful to have you here in this journey.

I also want to thank Joya Williams, who is also a part of this book. For her support in being another set of eyes editing the book further, to help it get publish ready. I am grateful for your support.

Of course I am always forever grateful for my family, whom whenever I take on a new project, like this book, had to share my attention and focus. Thank you for being my constant love.

For my kids, I love you. You are the reason why I do what I do. I am a better woman because of you. And to my husband Joel, thank you for being the stability in my very busy life. I love you!

And for you, dear reader, may you always have the courage to change what no longer serves you. Thank you for taking the time to read this book and allow these incredible women to share their stories with you.